QUICK & EASY
RECIPES
WITH JUST 4 INGREDIENTS

QUICK & EASY
RECIPES
WITH JUST 4 INGREDIENTS

METRO BOOKS
New York

METRO BOOKS
New York

An Imprint of Sterling Publishing
387 Park Avenue South
New York, NY 10016

ISBN 978-1-4351-3820-9

For information about custom editions, special sales, and premium and corporate purchases, please contact Sterling Special Sales at 800-805-5489 or specialsales@sterlingpublishing.com.

Manufactured in China

2 4 6 8 10 9 7 5 3 1

www.sterlingpublishing.com

contents

Breakfast

Often regarded as the most important meal of the day, this super-easy collection will help you serve relaxing morning breakfasts that work just as well for brunch.

34

strawberries and mint in orange syrup

1 orange
2 tablespoons brown sugar
1 pound strawberries, hulled and quartered
¼ cup coarsely chopped fresh mint

prep + cook time 10 minutes
serves 4

1 Grate zest from orange (you need 2 teaspoons); juice orange (you need 2 tablespoons).
2 Stir sugar and ¼ cup water in small saucepan, over low heat, until sugar dissolves; bring to the boil. Boil, uncovered, without stirring, about 3 minutes or until syrup thickens slightly. Remove from heat.
3 Stir zest and juice into syrup; cool. Combine strawberries and mint in medium bowl with syrup. Divide among serving dishes; serve with crème fraîche, if desired.

rhubarb, muesli and yogurt cups

2 cups coarsely chopped fresh or frozen rhubarb
¼ cup sugar
1⅓ cups vanilla yogurt
⅓ cup granola

prep + cook time
20 minutes (plus refrigeration time)
serves 4

1 Combine rhubarb, sugar and ½ cup water in medium saucepan; bring to boil. Reduce heat; simmer, uncovered, stirring occasionally, about 10 minutes or until rhubarb is tender. Transfer to medium heatproof bowl, cover; refrigerate 1 hour.
2 Divide mixture among four ¾-cup serving glasses; top with yogurt then granola.

strawberries and mint in orange syrup

tip These days many berries come packaged in clear plastic containers. Turn the container over and check the berries at bottom as they can become moldy. Berries don't ripen once they're picked, so the deeply colored ones tend to be the sweetest and most flavourful.

rhubarb, muesli and yogurt cups

tip Make the rhubarb the day before, if you like. Keep it, covered, in the fridge, so all you have to do is spoon everything into the serving glasses. Rhubarb stalks are the only edible portion of the plant—the leaves contain a toxic substance and should not be eaten.

roasted rhubarb and cranberries

2 pounds rhubarb, trimmed,
coarsely chopped
¼ cup dried cranberries
¼ cup brown sugar
1 tablespoon orange juice

prep + cook time 25 minutes
serves 4

1 Preheat oven to 350°F (325°F convection).
2 Combine ingredients in medium shallow baking
dish. Roast, uncovered, about 20 minutes or
until rhubarb is just tender.

spiced plums with yogurt

3 cans (15 ounces) whole
plums
2 cinnamon sticks
6 cardamom pods
1 cup Greek-style yogurt

prep + cook time 15 minutes
serves 6

1 Drain the juice from plums into medium
saucepan. Add spices to the pan; bring to the
boil. Reduce heat, simmer, uncovered,
3 minutes.
2 Remove from heat. Add plums to juice mixture;
cover pan, stand 10 minutes. Serve warm
plums with yogurt; drizzle with juice mixture.

roasted rhubarb and cranberries

tip Try serving
this delicious fruit
dish with a few good
dollops of sweetened
mascarpone cheese or
vanilla yogurt.

spiced plums with yogurt

tip Cardamom is
a spice native to India
that has a distinctive
aromatic, sweetly rich
flavor. It is used to
flavor curries, rice
dishes, sweet desserts
and cakes.

berry delicious

1 pound frozen mixed berries
¼ cup sugar
1 vanilla bean
⅔ cup Greek-style yogurt

prep + cook time 10 minutes
(+ refrigeration) **serves** 8

1 Combine berries and sugar in medium saucepan.
Split vanilla bean, scrape seeds into berry
mixture; add bean to pan. Cook over medium
heat about 3 minutes, stirring occasionally,
or until berries begin to soften. Cool.

2 Transfer berry mixture to container, cover;
refrigerate overnight.

3 Discard vanilla bean; serve berries with yogurt.

minted melon salad

4 pounds mixed melons
¼ cup loosely packed
fresh mint
½ cup apple juice

prep time 20 minutes
serves 8

1 Discard seeds from melons. Using melon
baller, cut balls of melon into large bowl.
Stir in mint and juice.

tip Berries are not only delicious, but they are also mega-healthy. They are loaded with antioxidants and contain a host of essential vitamins.

berry delicious

tip We used cantaloupe, honeydew and watermelon. If you don't have a melon baller, just cut the melons into pieces with a knife.

minted melon salad

yogurt with dried fruit and coconut

2 tablespoons finely chopped dried apricots

2 tablespoons finely chopped raisins

2 teaspoons sweetened coconut flakes

3/4 cup yogurt

prep time 5 minutes
serves 1

1 Combine fruit and coconut in small bowl. Place yogurt in serving bowl; sprinkle with apricot mixture.

ricotta and banana on toast

2 tablespoons ricotta cheese

2 slices rye bread, toasted

2 small bananas, thickly sliced

1 teaspoon honey

prep + cook time 10 minutes
serves 2

1 Divide cheese between toast slices; top with banana then drizzle with honey.

perfect oatmeal

1½ cups rolled oats
½ cup milk
2 tablespoons brown sugar
1 teaspoon ground cinnamon

prep + cook time 10 minutes
serves 4

1 Combine oats and 3½ cups hot water in medium saucepan over medium heat; cook, stirring, about 5 minutes or until oatmeal is thick and creamy.
2 Stir in milk. Serve oatmeal sprinkled with combined sugar and cinnamon.

granola and honey yogurt

⅓ cup yogurt
1 teaspoon honey
⅓ cup granola
2 tablespoons dried cranberries

prep time 5 minutes
serves 1

1 Combine yogurt and honey in small bowl. Combine granola and cranberries in another small bowl.
2 Layer yogurt mixture and granola in serving glass. Serve immediately.

bran and cranberry muesli

1 cup rolled oats
¾ cup all-bran cereal
¼ cup dried cranberries
½ cup fresh blueberries

prep time 5 minutes
serves 2

1 Combine oats, bran and cranberries in small bowl to make muesli mixture.
2 Serve muesli topped with berries

Serve with milk or yogurt.
Store remaining muesli in an airtight container.

granola bars

1 stick butter, coarsely chopped
½ cup firmly packed brown sugar
4 cups natural muesli
½ cup self-rising flour

prep + cook time 35 minutes
makes 30

1 Preheat oven to 375°F (350°F convection). Coat a 9 x 3 inch baking pan with cooking spray; line base and long sides with parchment paper, extending paper 2 inches over sides.
2 Heat butter and sugar in medium saucepan; stir until sugar dissolves. Stir in muesli and flour.
3 Press mixture firmly into pan; bake about 20 minutes. Let cool in pan before cutting.

Muesli, a combination of rolled oats and dried fruit, is available in gourmet grocery stores and health food stores

bran and cranberry muesli

granola bars

tip Dried cranberries, or craisins as they are commercially known, are a tart and delicious addition to this already healthy breakfast.

tip Use a muesli that contains nuts, dried fruit and coconut for maximum flavor and crunch.

cheesy scrambled eggs with spinach

8 eggs
⅓ cup spreadable cream cheese
1 cup baby spinach leaves, coarsely chopped

prep + cook time 10 minutes
serves 4

1 Whisk eggs in medium bowl until combined then whisk in cheese and spinach.
2 Cook mixture, stirring gently, in heated oiled skillet, over low heat, until set. Serve with whole wheat toast, if desired.

scrambled eggs with asparagus

¼ pounds asparagus, trimmed
4 eggs
2 tablespoons skim milk
1 small tomato, finely chopped

prep + cook time 15 minutes
serves 2

1 Boil, steam or microwave asparagus until tender; drain
2 Whisk eggs and milk in medium bowl. Cook egg mixture in oiled skillet, over low heat, stirring, until set.
3 Serve asparagus and scrambled eggs sprinkled with tomato.

Scrambled eggs need to be cooked and stirred gently until they are creamy and barely cooked. Over-cooking will toughen them. Serve at once or they'll become watery.

blt on croissant

12 slices bacon
4 large croissants
2 small tomatoes, thinly sliced
8 large butter lettuce leaves

prep + cook time 15 minutes
serves 4

1 Preheat broiler.
2 Cook bacon in large skillet until crisp.
3 Toast croissants under broiler about 30 seconds. Split croissants in half; top with bacon, tomato, lettuce and remaining croissant half.

huevos rancheros

1 small red onion
1 can (15 ounce) Mexican-flavored chopped tomatoes
4 eggs
4 corn tortillas, warmed

prep + cook time 30 minutes
serves 4

1 Cook onion in heated oiled large skillet, stirring, until softened. Add tomatoes; bring to the boil. Reduce heat; simmer, uncovered, 10 minutes, stirring occasionally, or until thickened.
2 Use a mixing spoon to make four shallow depressions into tomato mixture. Break one egg into a cup then slide egg into one of the hollows in tomato mixture; repeat with remaining eggs. Cover pan; cook over low heat, about 5 minutes or until eggs are set.
3 Divide warmed tortillas among plates. Use a serving spoon to carefully lift egg and tomato mixture onto each tortilla.

tomato and egg muffin

2 eggs
2 English muffins, split
1 small tomato, thinly sliced
2 teaspoons balsamic vinegar

prep + cook time 10 minutes
serves 2

1 Fry eggs in oiled medium skillet until cooked as you like them.
2 Meanwhile, toast muffins.
3 Divide tomato between two muffin halves; sprinkle with vinegar, top with eggs, then remaining muffin halves.

poached eggs with bacon and pecorino

1 pound spinach, trimmed, coarsely chopped
¼ pound bacon
4 eggs
⅓ cup shaved pecorino cheese

prep + cook time 15 minutes
serves 4

1 Boil, steam or microwave spinach until just wilted; drain. Cover to keep warm.
2 Meanwhile, cook bacon in heated large skillet until crisp. Transfer bacon to a plate lined with paper towels; cover to keep warm. Drain fat from skillet.
3 Half-fill same skillet with water; bring to boil. Break one egg into a cup then slide into pan. When all eggs are in skillet, allow water to return to boil. Cover skillet, turn off heat; stand about 4 minutes or until a light film of egg white sets over yolks. Remove eggs from pan, one at a time, using slotted spoon; place on paper towels to blot up poaching liquid.
4 Divide spinach among serving plates; top with bacon, egg then cheese.

tomato and egg muffin

tip You could also use hot sauce here instead of balsamic vinegar, if you like a spicier breakfast.

poached eggs with bacon and pecorino

tip Make sure you time the poaching of the eggs. Ideally, you want the egg yolk to be runny and starting to harden around the edges. It will burst open when you cut it, adding to the wonderful combination of flavors and textures.

eggs with tomato and basil

2 tablespoons olive oil

2 pounds tomatoes, coarsely chopped

1 cup coarsely chopped fresh basil

8 eggs

prep + cook time 20 minutes
serves 4

1 Heat oil in large skillet; cook tomato, stirring, 10 minutes or until thick and pulpy. Stir in basil.

2 Use a spoon to make eight shallow depressions into tomato mixture. Break one egg into a cup, then slide egg into one of the hollows in tomato mixture. Repeat with remaining eggs. Cover pan; cook over low heat about 5 minutes or until eggs are set.

3 Use a serving spoon to carefully lift egg and tomato mixture onto each serving plate. Serve with crusty bread, if desired.

egg-white omelette

We used chives, chervil and parsley in this recipe.

12 egg whites

1 cup finely chopped fresh mixed herbs

½ cup coarsely grated Cheddar cheese

½ cup coarsely grated mozzarella cheese

prep + cook time 45 minutes
serves 4

1 Preheat broiler.

2 Beat 3 egg whites in small bowl with electric mixer until soft peaks form; fold in a quarter of the herbs.

3 Pour mixture into heated oiled 5-inch ovenproof skillet; cook, uncovered, over low heat until omelette is just browned lightly on the bottom.

4 Sprinkle a quarter of the combined cheeses over half the omelette. Place pan under broiler until cheese begins to melt and omelette sets; fold omelette in half to completely cover cheese. Carefully slide onto serving plate; cover to keep warm.

5 Repeat process with remaining egg whites, herbs and cheese to make three more omelettes.

cheese and corn omelette

Add a bit of crisp bacon or even a few pan-fried mushrooms to the omelette, if you like.

8 eggs
1 can (15 ounce) creamed corn
¼ cup finely chopped fresh flat-leaf parsley
½ cup coarsely grated Cheddar cheese

prep + cook time 30 minutes
serves 4

1 Whisk eggs in medium bowl until combined; stir in remaining ingredients.
2 Pour a quarter of the egg mixture into heated oiled small skillet; cook over medium heat until omelette is set. Fold omelette in half, slide onto plate; cover to keep warm.
3 Repeat process with remaining egg mixture to make four omelettes.

smoked salmon and mascarpone omelette

8 eggs
½ cup mascarpone cheese
¼ pound sliced smoked salmon
2 tablespoons finely chopped fresh chervil

prep + cook time 25 minutes
serves 4

1 Whisk eggs with 2 tablespoons of the cheese in medium bowl until combined.
2 Oil small 5-inch skillet; heat over medium heat. Pour a quarter of the egg mixture into pan. Cook, tilting pan, until omelette is set.
3 Top half the omelette with a quarter of the salmon, a quarter of the chervil and a quarter of the remaining cheese. Fold omelette in half to enclose filling; slide onto serving plate.
4 Repeat to make three more omelettes.

ham, egg and cheese sandwich

2 slices whole wheat bread
1 ounce shaved ham
1 hard-boiled egg, thinly sliced
¼ cup coarsely grated Cheddar
   cheese

prep + cook time 10 minutes
serves 1

1 Preheat sandwich press.
2 Arrange ham, egg and cheese between
   bread slices.
3 Toast in sandwich press until golden brown.
   Serve with barbecue sauce, if desired.

baked eggs and bacon

2 slices bacon rashers, finely
   chopped
2 eggs
2 slices rye bread, toasted
1 small tomato, finely chopped

prep + cook time 20 minutes
serves 2

1 Preheat oven to 400°F (375°F convection).
2 Divide bacon between two ⅓-cup (80ml)
   muffin pan holes. If using a silicon tray, place
   on baking sheet before filling. Crack an egg
   into each hole. Bake about 15 minutes or until
   egg is set. Loosen edge of eggs from pan
   before releasing.
3 Serve eggs on toast; sprinkle with tomato.

ham, egg and cheese sandwich

tip Save time in the morning with this quick make-and-take breakfast. Boil some eggs on the weekend and use a conventional toaster and microwave oven to warm your ingredients if you don't have a sandwich press handy.

baked eggs and bacon

tip Silicone muffin cups are perfect for making baked eggs like these, as you can easily flip them out of the tray. If you don't have a silicone muffin tray, you should generously coat the pan holes with cooking spray before adding the bacon and egg, otherwise getting them out may be difficult.

roast vegetable frittata

6 eggs
½ cup light cream
⅓ cup coarsely grated Cheddar
  cheese
1½ cups coarsely chopped
  leftover roasted vegetables

prep + cook time 45 minutes
serves 4

1 Preheat oven to 350°F (325°F convection).
  Coat an 8 x 8 baking pan with cooking spray;
  line bottom and sides with parchment paper,
  extending paper 2 inches above edges.
2 Whisk eggs, cream and cheese in large bowl.
  Place vegetables in pan; pour egg mixture
  over vegetables.
3 Bake about 30 minutes or until frittata is set;
  stand in pan 10 minutes before lifting frittata
  out of pan to cut.

We used leftover roasted sweet potato, red
onion, zucchini and bell pepper in this recipe,
but any combination of roasted vegetables
are suitable to use.

bacon and asparagus frittata

½ pound center-cut bacon,
  coarsely chopped
¼ pound asparagus, trimmed,
  halved lengthways
6 eggs
¾ cup buttermilk

prep + cook time 50 minutes
serves 4

1 Preheat oven to 350°F (325°F convection).
  Coat an 8 x 8 baking pan with cooking spray;
  line bottom and sides with parchment paper,
  extending paper 2 inches above edges.
2 Cook bacon, stirring, in small skillet until
  crisp; drain on paper towels. Layer bacon and
  asparagus in prepared pan.
3 Whisk eggs and buttermilk in medium bowl;
  pour into pan. Bake, uncovered, in oven,
  about 35 minutes or until frittata is set.
  Stand in pan 10 minutes before lifting frittata
  out of pan to cut.

green bean and pesto frittata

1 pound green beans, trimmed,
  coarsely chopped
10 eggs
⅓ cup basil pesto
½ cup grated Parmesan cheese

prep + cook time 30 minutes
serves 4

1 Heat a large ovenproof skillet; cook beans, covered, stirring occasionally, until just tender.
2 Whisk eggs lightly in large bowl; whisk in pesto. Pour egg mixture over beans; sprinkle with cheese. Cook frittata, uncovered, over low heat until almost set.
3 Meanwhile, preheat broiler. Place pan under broiler until cheese melts. Remove from heat; stand frittata 10 minutes before serving.

pea and ricotta frittata

1½ cups frozen peas
 6 eggs
 2 tablespoons sour cream
 1 cup ricotta cheese

prep + cook time 35 minutes
serves 8

1 Preheat oven to 400°F. (375°F convection)
2 Add peas to small saucepan of boiling water; return to a boil, drain.
3 Combine eggs, sour cream, half the cheese and half the peas in large bowl.
4 Heat a large oiled ovenproof skillet; add egg mixture. Cook until base is set; transfer skillet to oven. Bake frittata about 12 minutes or until set and browned lightly.
5 Top frittata with remaining cheese and peas; place under preheated broiler until cheese is slightly melted. Serve frittata cut into wedges.

You can eat frittata hot, warm or at room temperature. Make it in advance and cut it just before serving so it doesn't dry out.

hash browns

2 pounds potatoes, unpeeled
1 small onion, finely chopped
2 teaspoons finely chopped
   fresh rosemary
4 tablespoons clarified butter

prep + cook time 40 minutes
makes 12

1 Boil, steam or microwave potatoes until just tender; drain. Cool 10 minutes.
2 Peel potatoes; cut into ½-inch cubes. Combine potato in large bowl with onion and rosemary.
3 Heat a third of the butter in a heavy skillet; place four egg rings in pan. Spoon ¼ cup of the potato mixture into each egg ring; using spatula, spread mixture evenly to fill ring. Cook, pressing frequently with spatula, until browned; carefully turn each ring to brown other side. Drain on paper towels; cover to keep warm.
4 Repeat step 3 to make a total of 12 hash browns.

buttermilk scones

2½ cups self-rising flour
1 tablespoon sugar
2 tablespoons butter
1¼ cups buttermilk,
   approximately

prep + cook time 35 minutes
makes 16

1 Preheat oven to 425°F (400°F convection). Coat an 8 x 8 baking pan with butter.
2 Sift flour and sugar into large bowl; rub in butter with fingertips.
3 Make well in center of flour mixture; add buttermilk. Using a knife, "cut" the buttermilk through the flour mixture to form a soft, sticky dough. Knead on floured surface until smooth.
4 Press dough out to a ¾-inch thickness. Dip 1¾-inch cutter into flour; cut as many rounds as you can from the piece of dough. Place scones side by side, just touching, in pan. Knead scraps of dough together; repeat pressing and cutting. Place in same pan. Brush tops with a little extra buttermilk.
5 Bake scones about 15 minutes or until browned.

hash browns

tip Clarified butter, also known as ghee, is regular butter without the milk solids that can burn at higher temperatures. To make clarified butter, heat a slice of butter in a small saucepan until the solids turn brown and separate by falling to the bottom. Transfer the clear liquid to a container and refrigerate until ready to use.

buttermilk scones

tip This is a fool-proof scone recipe—it's particularly good for beginners as they always turn out well. The buttermilk gives the scones a lovely texture and lightness. Perfectly cooked scones sound hollow when tapped firmly on top with fingers.

blueberry scones

2 cups self-rising flour
2 tablespoons confectioners' sugar
1¼ cups buttermilk
1 cup blueberries

prep + cook time 30 minutes
makes 8

1 Preheat oven to 475°F (450°F convection). Coat an 8-inch round cake pan with cooking spray.
2 Sift flour and sugar into large bowl; pour in enough buttermilk to mix to a sticky dough. Fold in blueberries.
3 Gently knead dough on floured surface until smooth; use hand to flatten out dough to about a 1-inch thickness. Cut eight 2¼-inch rounds from dough; place rounds, slightly touching, in pan.
4 Bake scones about 20 minutes or until browned; turn onto wire rack.

strawberry conserve

3 pounds strawberries, hulled
5 cups sugar
1 cup lemon juice

prep + cook time 1 hour 10 minutes (+ cooling)
makes 6 cups

1 Place strawberries in large saucepan; heat gently, covered, 5 minutes to extract juice from berries. Carefully remove berries from pan with slotted spoon, place in large bowl; reserve.
2 Add sugar and lemon juice to berry juice in pan, stir over heat, without boiling, until sugar dissolves; bring to a boil. Boil, uncovered, without stirring, 20 minutes. Return berries to pan; simmer, uncovered, without stirring, about 25 minutes or until jam gels. Pour jam into hot sterilized jars; seal.

apple and passionfruit jelly

5 apples, coarsely chopped
4 cups sugar, approximately
½ cup passionfruit pulp

prep + cook time 1 hour 25 minutes
(+ cooling)
makes 3 cups

1 Combine apple (seeds, skin, cores and all) and 6 cups of water in large saucepan; bring to a boil. Simmer, covered, 1 hour. Strain mixture through fine cloth; discard apple pulp.
2 Allow 1 cup of sugar for each cup of apple liquid.
3 Combine apple liquid and sugar in large saucepan. Stir over heat, without boiling, until sugar dissolves; bring to a boil. Boil, uncovered, 15 minutes or until jelly sets. Stir in passionfruit pulp.
4 Pour into hot sterilized jars; seal.

You need 6 passionfruit for this recipe.

quince jelly

6 large quinces (about
   4 pounds)
5 cups sugar, approximately
½ cup lemon juice, strained

prep + cook time 1 hour 40 minutes
(+ standing)
makes about 5 cups

Store jelly in a cool, dark place for up to 12 months. Refrigerate jelly once opened.

1 Chop unpeeled, uncored quinces coarsely.
2 Combine quince and 7 cups of water in large saucepan, bring to a boil; reduce heat, simmer, covered, about 1 hour or until quince is soft.
3 Strain mixture through fine cloth; stand overnight. Allow liquid to drip through cloth slowly, do not squeeze cloth; discard pulp.
4 Measure quince liquid. Allow 1 cup of sugar for each cup of quince liquid.
5 Combine quince liquid and sugar in large saucepan. Stir over heat, without boiling, until sugar is dissolved. Stir in juice, bring to a boil; boil, uncovered, without stirring, 25 minutes or until jelly sets when tested on a cold saucer.
6 Pour jelly into hot sterilized jars; seal while hot.

mixed berry and mascarpone brioche

1 cup heavy cream
6 ounces mascarpone cheese
4 thick slices brioche
½ pound mixed fresh berries

prep + cook time 10 minutes
serves 4

1 Beat cream in small bowl with electric mixer until soft peaks form; fold in cheese.
2 Preheat broiler. Toast brioche, both sides, under broiler. Place one brioche slice on each serving plate; spread with cheese mixture then top with berries. Serve sprinkled with a little finely chopped fresh mint and dust with sifted confectioners' sugar, if desired.

waffles with maple syrup and strawberries

8 packaged belgian-style waffles
1 tablespoon butter
1 pound strawberries, hulled and sliced
½ cup pure maple syrup

prep + cook time 25 minutes
serves 4

1 Preheat oven to 325°F (300°F convection).
2 Place waffles, in single layer, on oven tray; heat, uncovered, about 8 minutes.
3 Meanwhile, melt butter in medium saucepan, add strawberries; cook, stirring gently, about 2 minutes or until just heated through. Add maple syrup; cook, stirring gently, until heated through.
4 Divide waffles among serving plates; top with strawberry-maple mixture and a dollop of vanilla yogurt or whipped cream, if desired.

tip Mascarpone is not for the diet conscious. It's a triple-cream cheese made from cows milk, and is one of the key ingredients in the Italian dessert Tiramisu.

mixed berry and mascarpone brioche

tip You can find frozen Belgian-style waffles in most supermarkets shelves and at most delicatessens. They are a thick, crispy and fluffy waffle made with a yeast batter.

waffles with maple syrup and strawberries

berry smoothie

½ pound strawberries
½ cup blueberries
1 cup skim milk
¾ cup skim-milk
    fruit-flavored yogurt

prep time 5 minutes
serves 2

1 Blend ingredients until smooth.

*You can use either fresh or frozen blueberries
in the smoothie.*

watermelon, berry and mint frappé

¾ pound seedless watermelon,
    coarsely chopped
¼ pound strawberries
1 tablespoon lime juice
20 ice cubes, crushed

prep time 5 minutes
serves 2

1 Blend or process watermelon, berries and juice
until smooth; transfer to serving glasses.
Stir in ice.

tip To make this a more filling breakfast smoothie you could add a few spoonfuls of toasted oats!

berry smoothie

tip A frappé is best made just before serving as the thick, creamy texture will subside and separate if it stands for too long.

watermelon, berry and mint frappé

34

Snacks and Starters

Whipping up a quick snack or first course to a great meal doesn't mean you have to sacrifice taste or nutrition. Here are some palate-pleasing options to expand your repertoire of simple meals.

pear with cheese and prosciutto

2 pears, unpeeled

2 teaspoons lemon juice

4 ounces blue cheese, crumbled

6 slices prosciutto, halved lengthways

1 Cut each pear into 6 wedges; remove and discard core from each wedge. Sprinkle wedges with juice.

2 Press cheese over prosciutto slices. Wrap prosciutto firmly around each pear wedge.

prep time 15 minutes
makes 12

figs with prosciutto

6 large black figs (about 1 pound), halved

6 slices prosciutto, halved

3 teaspoons balsamic vinegar

1 Arrange figs on serving platter, top with prosciutto. Drizzle figs with vinegar and sprinkle with pepper.

prep time 5 minutes
makes 12

pear with cheese and prosciutto

tip Blue cheese varieties range from firm and crumbly stilton types to mild, creamy brie-like cheeses. Use a firm and crumbly blue cheese for this recipe.

tips Recipe is best made just before serving. Figs are at their best during Autumn. Choose ripe, sweet-smelling fruit.

figs with prosciutto

potato chips with spicy salt

3 pounds mixed sweet potato, white potato and purple potato

2 teaspoons sea salt

½ teaspoon red pepper flakes

½ teaspoon sweet paprika

prep + cook time 25 minutes
serves 4

1 Using vegetable peeler, slice potatoes into long, thin strips.

2 Deep-fry sweet potato strips in wok of hot oil, in batches, until browned lightly and crisp. Drain on wire rack over paper towel-lined tray.

3 Combine salt, pepper flakes and paprika in small bowl. Sprinkle hot chips with chilli salt mixture.

jerusalem artichoke chips

2 pounds jerusalem artichokes, unpeeled, thinly sliced

2 tablespoons olive oil

1 teaspoon salt

½ teaspoon cracked black pepper

prep + cook time 30 minutes
serves 4

1 Preheat oven to 400°F (375°F convection).

2 Combine ingredients in medium bowl; place artichoke slices, in single layer, on wire rack over large baking dish. Roast about 20 minutes or until crisp.

potato chips with spicy salt

tip We used white and purple potatoes along with sweet potatoes here for a mix of colors and flavors. The orange sweet potato tends to require slightly longer frying time than the other two, so for best results, deep-fry the sweet potato separately first.

jerusalem artichoke chips

tip Jerusalem artichokes have a knobbly, uneven surface that hides their creamy, smooth consistency on the inside. They have a delicious and distinctively nutty taste, and a crisp and crunchy texture that is similar to a water chestnut.

roasted pepper and walnut dip

½ cup finely chopped walnuts
2 medium red bell peppers
8 ounces cream cheese

prep + cook time 35 minutes
makes 2 cups

1 Toast walnuts in a small dry skillet over medium-high heat until fragrant..
2 Preheat broiler.
3 Quarter bell peppers; discard seeds and membranes. Cook bell peppers, skin-side up, until skin blisters and blackens. Transfer peppers to a glass bowl; cover with plastic or paper for 5 minutes then peel away skin; chop coarsely.
4 Blend or process bell peppers and cream cheese until smooth; stir in nuts.

Serve with celery sticks or crackers.

roasted cherry tomato and parmesan dip

1 pint cherry tomatoes
½ cup sour cream
½ cup grated Parmesan cheese
2 tablespoons finely chopped fresh basil

prep + cook time 35 minutes
serves 6

1 Preheat oven to 425°F (400°F convection).
2 Place tomatoes on baking sheet; lightly coat with oil-spray. Roast, uncovered, about 15 minutes or until tomato skins split. Cool 10 minutes.
3 Combine tomatoes, sour cream, cheese and basil in medium bowl.

Serve with toasted garlic bread.

pita chips with eggplant dip

1 package plain pita chips
8 ounces prepared eggplant dip
¾ cup walnut halves
½ cup fresh mint

prep time 10 minutes
serves 6

1 Toast walnuts in small dry skillet over medium-high heat until fragrant.
2 Top each chip with a teaspoon of eggplant dip, half a toasted walnut and a mint leaf. Serve on platter; drizzle with olive oil, if desired.

curried egg dip

4 hard-boiled eggs, coarsely chopped
¼ cup mayonnaise
1 teaspoon curry powder
2 tablespoons finely chopped fresh chives

prep + cook time 15 minutes
makes about 1 cup

1 Combine eggs, mayonnaise, curry powder and half the chives in small bowl; season to taste. Sprinkle with remaining chives.

sweet chili cream cheese dip

8 ounces cream cheese,
  softened
½ cup sour cream
½ cup sweet chili sauce
¼ cup coarsely chopped
  fresh cilantro

prep time 10 minutes
makes 2 cups

1 Beat cream cheese, sour cream and sauce in small bowl with electric mixer until smooth. Stir in cilantro; season to taste.

pizza chips

20 large tortilla chips
¼ cup pizza sauce
20 thin slices pepperoni
2 ounces Cheddar cheese,
  cut into small cubes

prep + cook time 10 minutes
serves 4

1 Top chips with a little sauce, pepperoni and cheese; place on oven tray under preheated broiler until cheese melts.

sweet chili cream cheese dip

tip Leave the cream cheese to soften or if you haven't the time, cut it into cubes and beat it with an electric mixer before adding other ingredients. Sweet chili sauce is available in the Asian food section of most grocery stores.

pizza chips

tip Try salami instead of pepperoni, or for tex mex chips, use shredded barbecued chicken and tomato salsa.

tomato tarts

4 vine-ripened tomatoes,
  peeled, quartered, seeded
1 tablespoon brown sugar
1 tablespoon balsamic vinegar
½ sheet frozen, thawed puff
  pastry

prep + cook time 35 minutes
makes 16

1 Preheat oven 425°F (400°F convection).
2 Combine tomato, sugar and vinegar in
  small baking dish; roast, uncovered, about
  20 minutes or until tomato is soft.
3 Meanwhile, cut pastry sheet in half lengthways,
  cut each half into 4 squares; cut each square
  into triangles (you will have 16). Place pastry
  triangles on baking sheet lined with
  parchment paper. Coat the bottom side of
  another baking sheet with cooking spray and
  place on top (the second stops the pastry from
  puffing up). Bake pastry, alongside tomato,
  about 10 minutes or until crisp.
4 Place a tomato piece on each pastry triangle.

Serve topped with chervil.

fig and feta toasts

4 ounces marinated feta
1 tablespoon finely chopped
  fresh chives
24 melba toasts
3 medium fresh figs

prep time 10 minutes
makes 24

1 Using fork, mash feta with chives in small
  bowl; spread on one side of each toast.
2 Cut each fig into eight wedges; place one
  wedge on each toast. Sprinkle with coarsely
  ground black pepper, if desired.

tomato tarts

tip These tarts are best made immediately before serving to prevent the pastry from becoming soggy. You can pre-roast the tomatoes ahead of time, but don't assemble the tarts until just before serving.

fig and feta toasts

tips You can purchase marinated feta in the refrigerated cheese section of supermarkets. Or, try making your own by placing feta in a small jar with peeled garlic cloves, dried oregano and red pepper flakes, before covering with extra virgin olive oil. Refrigerate for at least 24 hours before using.

asparagus and brie bruschetta

¾ pound asparagus spears, trimmed

3 cloves garlic, thinly sliced

1 Turkish bread loaf

4 ounces thinly sliced brie cheese

prep + cook time 30 minutes

serves 4

1 Preheat oven to 400°F (375°F convection).
2 Combine asparagus and garlic in large baking dish that has been coated with cooking spray. Roast, uncovered, 10 minutes.
3 Meanwhile, cut bread crossways into 6 pieces; place on baking sheet; bake 5 minutes.
4 Top bread with asparagus mixture and cheese; bake about 10 minutes or until cheese melts. Garnish with lemon thyme sprigs, if desired.

spinach and feta pinwheels

½ pound frozen spinach, thawed

4 ounces feta cheese, crumbled

½ cup finely grated Parmesan cheese

2 sheets frozen puff pastry, thawed

prep + cook time 30 minutes

makes 24

1 Preheat oven to 425°F (400°F convection). Line two baking sheets with parchment paper.
2 Squeeze excess moisture from spinach. Chop spinach coarsely; pat dry between sheets of paper towels.
3 Sprinkle spinach and combined cheeses over pastry sheets. Roll pastry tightly to enclose filling. Cut each roll into 12 slices.
4 Place pinwheels, cut-side up, on trays; bake about 15 minutes or until lightly browned.

asparagus and brie bruschetta

spinach and feta pinwheels

pigs in blankets

2 sheets frozen puff pastry, thawed

32 cocktail frankfurters

1 egg, beaten lightly

prep + cook time 40 minutes
serves 8

1 Preheat oven to 425°F (400°F convection).
2 Cut each pastry sheet into 16 squares; wrap a frankfurter in each square, brush with egg. Bake, on parchment paper-lined baking sheet, about 25 minutes or until pastry is puffed and golden.
3 Serve with ketchup, if desired.

For extra flavor, brush pastry with a little mustard before wrapping around sausage.

crostini with feta, artichokes and arugula

1 small loaf french bread

5 marinated artichoke hearts, drained

4 ounces marinated feta cheese

1 cup baby arugula

prep + cook time 20 minutes
serves 6

1 Preheat oven to 350°F (325°F convection).
2 To make crostini, slice bread into 3-inch-thick rounds; lightly spray both sides with olive oil-spray. Place on baking sheet; toast in oven, turning once, until lightly browned both sides.
3 Place crostini on serving platter. Cut each artichoke heart into six wedges. Drain cheese, reserving 2 tablespoons of the oil; crumble cheese. Top crostini with arugula then artichokes; sprinkle with cheese. Serve drizzled with reserved oil.

haloumi and tapenade toasts

1 small loaf french bread
¼ cup black olive tapenade
6 ounces haloumi cheese
2 tablespoons chopped fresh
   oregano

prep + cook time 25 minutes
makes 20

1 Cut bread into 20 thin slices. Toast slices under
  preheated broiler; spread with tapenade.
2 Cut cheese into 20 slices; cook in oiled frying
  pan until lightly browned on both sides. Top
  each toast with cheese; sprinkle with oregano.

*You can toast both sides of bread for a crunchy
toast, or only one side for a softer texture.*

blue cheese mini pizzas

1 12-inch ready-made pizza
   crust
2 tablespoons tomato paste
2 scallions, thinly sliced
3 ounces blue cheese, coarsely
   chopped

prep + cook time 30 minutes
makes 24

1 Preheat oven to 400°F (375°F convection).
2 Using 2-inch cutter, cut rounds from pizza
  crust.
3 Place rounds on baking sheet. Divide paste
  evenly among rounds; top with scallion and
  cheese. Bake about 5 minutes or until pizzas
  are heated through. Serve hot.

pizza caprese

2 (12-inch) pizza crusts with
   tomato paste
4 large roma tomatoes,
   thinly sliced
6 ounces bocconcini cheese,
   halved
¼ cup thinly sliced fresh basil

prep + cook time 25 minutes
serves 4

1 Preheat oven to 425°F (400°F convection).
  Coat two baking sheets with cooking spray.
2 Top pizzas with tomato and cheese. Bake,
  uncovered, about 15 minutes or until cheese
  is melted. Sprinkle pizzas with basil.

ham, sage and fontina pizza

2 (12-inch) pizza crusts
6 ounces fontina cheese,
   thinly sliced
2 tablespoons finely chopped
   fresh sage
3 ounces thinly sliced ham

prep + cook time 20 minutes
serves 4

1 Preheat oven to 420°F (400°F convection).
  Coat two baking sheets with cooking spray.
2 Top pizzas with half the cheese; sprinkle with
  sage then top with ham and remaining cheese.
  Bake, uncovered, about 15 minutes or until
  cheese is melted.

pizza caprese

ham, sage and fontina pizza

tip Commercial pizza crusts are available in a full range of thicknesses. For this pizza, select a thinner base so it complements rather than competes with the flavors of the topping.

tip Fontina is a classic Italian cows-milk cheese that has been made in the Aosta Valley, in the Alps, since the 12th century. It's very rich and creamy—with a milk fat content of around 45%—and has a nutty flavor that intensifies with age. Fontina can be replaced by gruyère, edam or gouda.

roasted eggplant and chorizo pizza

2 (12-inch) frozen cheese pizzas

1 jar (10-ounce) char-grilled eggplant in oil, drained, coarsely chopped

½ cup pitted kalamata olives

1 chorizo sausage (5 ounces), thinly sliced

prep + cook time 25 minutes
serves 4

1 Preheat oven to 425°F (400°F convection). Coat two baking sheets with cooking spray.

2 Top pizzas with eggplant, olives and chorizo. Bake, uncovered, about 15 minutes. Sprinkle pizzas with oregano, if desired.

grilled feta and tomatoes

6 ounces feta cheese

¾ pound baby cherry tomatoes

1 tablespoon extra virgin olive oil

1 teaspoon Greek oregano

prep + cook time 10 minutes
serves 4

1 Preheat broiler.

2 Place cheese and tomatoes on baking sheet. Drizzle with oil; sprinkle with oregano. Season with pepper. Place under broiler (about 8 inches away from heat) about 8 minutes or until cheese is golden and soft.

Serve with toasted french bread, if desired.

roasted eggplant and chorizo pizza

grilled feta and tomatoes

tip Chorizo sausage is a highly seasoned, coarsely-ground pork sausage flavored with garlic, smoked paprika and other spices. It's widely used in both Mexican and Spanish dishes. Mexican chorizo is made with fresh pork, while the Spanish version uses smoked pork.

tip Greek dried oregano is available from specialty supermarkets and Mediterranean food stores. Use regular dried oregano if you can't find it.

oven-baked feta

1 piece (6 ounces) feta cheese

1 tablespoon extra virgin olive oil

1 tablespoon coarsely chopped fresh oregano

¼ teaspoon sweet paprika

prep + cook time 15 minutes
serves 6

1 Preheat oven to 400°F (375°F convection).

2 Place cheese in small ovenproof dish; sprinkle with oil, oregano leaves and paprika. Bake, covered, about 10 minutes or until cheese is heated through.

baked brie

1 piece (6 ounces) brie cheese

2 sprigs fresh thyme

2 tablespoons dry red wine

1 teaspoon fresh lemon zest

prep + cook time 35 minutes
serves 8

1 Preheat oven to 400°F (375°F convection). Coat 1 cup ovenproof dish (4 inches diameter, 2 inches deep.)

2 Place cheese in dish; make six small slits into cheese. Cut 1 sprig thyme into six pieces; push thyme into slits. Remove leaves from remaining thyme sprig; finely chop.

3 Pour wine over cheese; cover dish; place on baking sheet. Bake about 20 minutes. Stand, covered, 5 minutes. Serve sprinkled with zest and finely chopped thyme sprig.

tip Oven-baked feta is a wonderfully simple and foolproof dish that is perfect for entertaining family and friends. You can whip it up quickly and serve it with toasted pita bread and black olives.

oven-baked feta

tip This velvety smooth and luxurious baked brie makes an elegant and impressive appetizer. The red wine not only gives it a beautiful deep red color but also adds a lovely richness to the dish. Serve it with sliced bread or crackers.

baked brie

deep-south wings

16 small chicken wings
¼ cup ketchup
¼ cup Worcestershire sauce
¼ cup light brown sugar

prep + cook time 40 minutes
(+ refrigeration)
serves 8

1 Preheat oven to 425°F (400°F convection).
2 Cut wings into three pieces at joints; discard tips. Combine chicken with remaining ingredients in large bowl. Cover; refrigerate 3 hours or overnight.
3 Place chicken, in single layer, on oiled wire rack set inside large shallow baking dish; brush remaining marinade over chicken. Roast about 30 minutes or until chicken is cooked through.
4 Serve wings with dipping sauce.

honey, soy and sesame chicken wings

2 pounds chicken wings
¼ cup japanese soy sauce
2 tablespoons honey
2 teaspoons sesame seeds

prep + cook time
45 minutes (plus refrigeration time)
serves 8

1 Cut chicken wings into three pieces at joints; discard tips. Combine sauce, honey and seeds in large bowl with chicken. Cover; refrigerate 3 hours or overnight.
2 Preheat oven to 425°F (400°F convection).
3 Place chicken, in single layer, on oiled wire rack over large shallow baking dish; brush chicken with any remaining marinade. Roast about 30 minutes or until chicken is cooked through.
4 Serve chicken wings sprinkled with sliced scallion, if desired.

lemon pepper chicken drumettes

24 chicken drumettes
(2 pounds)
2 teaspoons lemon pepper
seasoning
1 tablespoon olive oil
1/4 teaspoon ground turmeric

prep + cook time 35 minutes
serves 8

1 Preheat oven to 425°F (400°F convection).
Line large baking dish with parchment paper.
2 Combine chicken with remaining ingredients
in medium bowl.
3 Place chicken in dish, in single layer. Bake,
uncovered, about 30 minutes or until chicken
is cooked through. Cool.

*Chicken can be cooked, cooled and refrigerated a
day before the picnic.*

chicken tikka drumettes

12 chicken drumettes (1 pound)
1/3 cup tikka masala paste
1/2 cup yogurt
1/4 cup coarsely chopped
fresh cilantro

prep + cook time 30 minutes
serves 4

1 Preheat oven to 400°F (375°F convection).
2 Place chicken in large bowl with combined
paste and 2 tablespoons of the yogurt; toss to
coat chicken in paste mixture. Place chicken, in
single layer, on wire rack in large baking dish.
Roast, uncovered, about 30 minutes or until
chicken is browned and cooked through.
3 Combine cilantro and remaining yogurt in
small bowl. Serve chicken with yogurt mixture.

sticky chicken drumettes

¾ cup ketchup

⅓ cup plum sauce

2 tablespoons Worcestershire sauce

16 chicken drumettes

prep + cook time 35 minutes

serves 4

1 Preheat oven to 400°F (375°F convection).
2 Combine sauces in large bowl; add chicken, toss to combine.
3 Place chicken on oiled wire rack over large baking dish. Roast chicken about 30 minutes or until cooked through.

tandoori wings

16 small chicken wings

½ cup tandoori paste

½ cup yogurt

1 onion, coarsely grated

prep + cook time 40 minutes
(+ refrigeration)

serves 8

1 Preheat oven to 425°F (400°F convection).
2 Cut wings into three pieces at joints; discard tips. Combine remaining ingredients in large bowl, add chicken; toss chicken to coat in mixture. Cover; refrigerate 3 hours or overnight.
3 Place chicken, in single layer, on oiled wire rack set inside large shallow baking dish. Roast about 30 minutes or until chicken is well browned and cooked through.

Serve with lime wedges, if desired. You can also make this recipe with chicken drumettes if you find the wings too fatty.

sticky chicken drumettes

tandoori wings

tip These finger-licking-good chicken drumettes will be loved as much by the adults as by the kids. A drumette is just the first section of the wing, which has had the tip removed.

tip Tandoori paste is a classic East Indian spice paste usually containing a mixture of ginger, garlic, chili powder, garam masala, cumin and food coloring. It is used to give foods the red-orange tint of classical tandoor (round clay oven) cooking. Here it is mixed with yogurt and used as a marinade.

Lunch

Forget that same old sandwich you have every day. Be inspired to liven up your lunchbox with these flavor-packed meals.

egg and chive sandwich

2 hard-boiled eggs, halved

2 tablespoons ricotta cheese

2 tablespoons finely chopped
  fresh chives

4 slices rye bread

prep time 5 minutes
serves 2

1 Place egg, cheese and chives in medium bowl;
  using back of fork, crush until combined.
2 Sandwich egg mixture between bread slices.
  Cut as desired to serve.

blue cheese and fig bites

1 long turkish loaf

6 ounces semi-dried figs,
  thinly sliced

6 ounces blue cheese,
  thinly sliced

1 /3 cup toasted slivered almonds,

prep + cook time 20 minutes
serves 4

1 Preheat broiler.
2 Halve turkish loaf lengthways; cut each half
  lengthways into three fingers then cut fingers
  crossways into four to get 24 slices. Toast
  bread under broiler.
3 Top half the toasts with figs and cheese;
  sprinkle with nuts. Top with remaining toast.

egg and chive sandwich

tip For perfectly hard boiled eggs, place eggs in salted boiling water for 7 minutes and then drain. Immediately put them in cold water and stand a few minutes before peeling. It's worth doing a few at a time so you have some on hand for sandwiches, salads or just a simple snack.

blue cheese and fig bites

tip The sweetness of the figs matches beautifully with the tangy blue cheese. If figs are in season you could use fresh ones instead of dried.

curried egg sandwiches

4 hard-boiled eggs, halved
⅓ cup ricotta cheese
2 teaspoons curry powder
8 slices rye bread

1 Place eggs, cheese and curry powder in medium bowl; using back of fork, crush until combined.
2 Sandwich egg mixture between bread slices. Cut each sandwich into four triangles.

prep time 5 minutes
serves 4

carrot, raisin and cottage cheese sandwich

½ small carrot, coarsely grated
1 tablespoon cottage cheese
2 teaspoons raisins
2 slices white bread

1 Combine carrot, cheese and raisins in small bowl.
2 Sandwich cheese mixture between bread slices. Cut as desired to serve.

prep time 5 minutes
makes 1

cucumber sandwiches

½ English cucumber
  sea salt flakes
8 slices white bread
2 tablespoons butter, softened

prep time 10 minutes (+ standing)
serves 4

1 Peel cucumber; slice as thinly as possible. Place cucumber in a strainer or colander, sprinkle with salt; stand 20 minutes, then rinse cucumber with cold water, drain well. Pat dry with paper towels.
2 Spread bread with butter. Sandwich cucumber between bread slices.
3 Cut crusts from bread; cut each sandwich into three fingers to serve.

avocado, bacon and tomato panini

½ pound bacon
4 panini bread rolls
1 avocado, thinly sliced
2 tomatoes, thinly sliced

prep + cook time 15 minutes
serves 4

1 Cook bacon in heated oiled large skillet until crisp. Drain on paper towels.
2 Meanwhile, split and toast cut sides of bread rolls. Fill rolls with avocado, tomato and bacon.

Use ciabatta bread if panini rolls aren't available.

radish and onion sandwiches

6 tablespoons butter, softened
1 scallion, finely chopped
12 slices white bread
10 radishes, thinly sliced

prep time 30 minutes
makes 16

1 Combine butter and scallion in small bowl. Season to taste.
2 Spread butter mixture over one side of eight slices of bread and over both sides of four slices of bread.
3 Top four slices of the bread buttered on one side with half the radish; top with the bread buttered on both sides. Top with remaining radish and bread. Cut and discard crusts; cut each sandwich into four triangles.

salmon and onion sandwiches

1 can (15 ounces) red salmon, drained
¼ cup mayonnaise
12 scallions, finely chopped
8 slices white bread

prep time 20 minutes
serves 4

1 Discard any skin or bones from salmon. Combine salmon with mayonnaise and onion in medium bowl.
2 Divide salmon mixture among 4 slices of the bread; top with remaining bread slices.
3 Remove crusts; cut sandwiches into quarters.

radish and onion sandwiches

tip Remove butter from fridge 30 minutes before making sandwiches to bring it to room temperature and soften.

tip Sandwiches can be made up to 1 hour ahead. Cover; refrigerate until ready to serve.

salmon and onion sandwiches

smoked trout salad roll

½ pound flaked smoked trout

¼ cup light sour cream

1 tablespoon finely chopped fresh dill

4 whole-grain kaiser rolls, split in half

prep time 10 minutes
serves 4

1 Combine trout, sour cream and dill in small bowl. Sandwich rolls with filling.

ricotta, zucchini and ham wrap

2 small zucchini

¼ cup low-fat ricotta cheese

3 whole grain tortilla wraps

2 ounces shaved ham

prep + cook time 10 minutes
serves 2

1 Preheat sandwich press.
2 Slice zucchini lengthways into ribbons using a vegetable peeler.
3 Divide cheese among wraps; top with zucchini, and ham. Roll to enclose.
4 Toast wraps in sandwich press about 3 minutes.
5 Cut in half to serve.

smoked trout salad roll

tip Trout is an oil-rich fish high in all-important omega-3 polyunsaturated fatty acids, which are vital to heart health. Trout is low in fat and calories, and is a good source of iron, calcium and vitamins. Health experts recommend two servings of oil-rich fish each week.

ricotta, zucchini and ham wrap

tip Ricotta is a mild, soft, moist cow's-milk cheese with a low-fat content and a slightly grainy texture. It can be used in sweet and savory dishes alike, and is an excellent spread on sandwiches and a nice alternative to mayonnaise.

mexican chicken wraps

16 chicken tenderloins
1 packet (1 ounce) taco
  seasoning mix
8 large (10-inch) flour tortillas,
  halved
1 large avocado, mashed

prep + cook time 15 minutes
serves 8

1 Toss chicken in seasoning mix. Cook chicken
  in heated oiled grill pan over medium-high
  heat until cooked through.
2 Meanwhile, warm tortillas according to the
  packet directions.
3 Spread tortillas with avocado; top with
  chicken. Roll wraps to enclose filling.

*You can serve these wraps with sour cream and
lime wedges, if you like.*

chicken tandoori wrap

*You will need one large rotisserie
chicken for this recipe.*

3½ cups coarsely chopped
   cooked chicken
¼ cup tandoori paste
¾ cup yogurt
4 pieces lavash bread

prep + cook time 25 minutes
serves 4

1 Combine chicken, tandoori paste and ¼ cup
  of the yogurt in heated oiled medium skillet;
  cook, stirring, about 5 minutes or until hot.
2 Place a quarter of the chicken mixture along
  short side of one piece of lavash; drizzle
  with a quarter of the remaining yogurt,
  roll to enclose filling. Repeat with remaining
  ingredients to make three more wraps. Serve
  with mango chutney, if desired.

ham, cheese and spinach wraps

2 wholegrain tortilla wraps
1 cup baby spinach
¼ cup coarsely grated smoked
   Cheddar cheese
2 ounces shaved honey ham

1 Top wraps with spinach, cheese and ham; roll
to enclose.
2 Cut rolls into thirds crossways to serve.

prep time 15 minutes
serves 2

ham and mustard wraps

4 whole grain bread wraps
⅓ cup Dijon mustard
5 ounces shaved ham
¼ pound snow pea sprouts

1 Spread wraps with mustard; top with
remaining ingredients. Roll to enclose.

prep time 15 minutes
serves 4

turkey and cranberry wrap

2 whole grain tortilla wraps
2 tablespoons cranberry sauce
2 ounces shaved turkey
1 cup mixed salad greens

1 Spread wraps with sauce; top with remaining ingredients. Roll to enclose.
2 Cut as desired to serve.

prep time 5 minutes
serves 2

lamb, tabbouleh and hummus on pita

4 pocket pitas, split lengthways
⅓ cup hummus
1 cup tabbouleh
½ pound thinly sliced roast lamb

1 Spread pita with hummus; sandwich with tabbouleh and lamb. Cut in half to serve.

prep time 5 minutes
serves 4

tip Turkey and cranberry is a classic and delicious combination. For a little extra indulgence and creaminess add some sliced brie cheese.

turkey and cranberry wrap

tip Hummus is a dip made from chickpeas. In fact, hummus is the Arabic word for chickpea. It has been around for thousands of years and is eaten throughout the Middle East, the Mediterranean and in many parts of India (which is why it is spelled in so many ways—hoummos, hommos, hommus, homous), and is now popular around the world. Hummus is often eaten with pita bread or vegetables, and can be a heart-healthy spread on sandwiches.

lamb, tabbouleh and hummus on pita

smoked chicken mini rolls

6 ounces finely shredded
  smoked chicken
¼ cup basil pesto
⅓ cup mayonnaise
12 mini bread rolls

prep time 15 minutes
serves 4

1 Combine chicken, pesto and mayonnaise in
  medium bowl.
2 Make a cut in the tops of 12 mini bread rolls.
  Spoon chicken mixture into rolls.

chicken and celery sandwich

¼ cup finely shredded
  cooked chicken
½ trimmed celery stick, finely
  chopped
1 tablespoon mayonnaise
2 slices wholegrain bread

prep time 10 minutes
makes 1

1 Combine chicken, celery and mayonnaise in
  small bowl.
2 Spread one slice of bread with chicken
  mixture. Top with remaining bread slice.
  Cut as desired to serve.

sausage sandwiches

8 rosemary and garlic sausages (4 ounces each)
1 loaf Turkish bread
¾ cup prepared caramelized onion chutney
2 cups firmly packed watercress

prep + cook time 25 minutes
serves 4

1 Cook sausages in heated oiled large skillet until browned all over and cooked through. Cool. Halve sausages lengthways.
2 Meanwhile, split bread lengthways; spread base with chutney. Top with sausage halves and watercress; press lid on firmly. Wrap sandwich in plastic wrap or foil.

basic steak sandwich

1 pound beef tenderloin steaks
2 small loaves french bread
1 cup watercress
1 tablespoon prepared horseradish

prep + cook time 25 minutes
serves 4

1 Cook tenderloin in heated oiled skillet over medium-high heat until cooked as desired. Cover; stand 5 minutes then slice thinly.
2 Meanwhile, slice bread in half lengthways (do not cut all the way through), then cut each in half crossways. Fill each with equal amounts of watercress, beef and horseradish.

roast beef and coleslaw on rye

1 tablespoon prepared
  horseradish
¼ pound shaved rare roast beef
4 slices rye bread
½ cup prepared coleslaw

prep time 10 minutes
serves 2

1 Divide horseradish, beef and coleslaw and
  arrange between bread slices.
2 Cut as desired to serve.

lamb pockets with
baba ghanoush and arugula

1 pound boneless lamb loin
4 pita breads
8 ounces baba ghanoush
1 cup baby arugula

prep + cook time 15 minutes
serves 8

1 Cook lamb in heated, oiled large skillet over
  high heat until cooked as desired. Cover lamb;
  stand 10 minutes then slice lamb thinly.
2 Spread inside of pitas with baba ghanoush;
  fill with lamb and rocket.

roast beef and coleslaw on rye

tip Coleslaw is a great crunchy addition to sandwiches. It can have just about anything in it as long as shredded cabbage is the chief ingredient. Most coleslaws also have grated carrot and a mayonnaise or vinegar (or both) dressing.

lamb pockets with baba ghanoush and arugula

tip Baba ghanoush is a classic Middle Eastern eggplant spread. It has a deliciously smoky and garlicky flavor and a creamy texture.

Soup and salad

Make the most of fresh, seasonal ingredients. From lush and creamy soups to crunchy summer salads, these delicious dishes are nutritious and packed full of flavor.

34

spiced squash and coconut soup

1 pound butternut squash, peeled and chopped coarsely
1 can (15 ounces) coconut cream
1 small sweet potato, chopped coarsely
1 tablespoon curry powder

prep + cook time 30 minutes
serves 4

1 Reserve ½ cup coconut cream. Combine remaining coconut cream, squash, sweet potato, curry powder and 3 cups water in large saucepan. Bring to a boil; reduce heat, simmer, uncovered, 10 minutes or until vegetables are soft.
2 Stand 10 minutes then blend or process mixture, in batches, until smooth.
3 Meanwhile, heat reserved coconut cream in small saucepan without boiling. Serve soup drizzled with coconut cream.

tomato and bell pepper soup

2 can (15 ounces) diced tomatoes
1⅓ cups drained char-grilled bell peppers
3 cups chicken stock
1 can (15 ounces) cannellini beans, rinsed, drained

prep + cook time 30 minutes
serves 4

1 Combine undrained tomato, bell peppers and half the stock in large saucepan; bring to a boil. Reduce heat; simmer, covered, about 20 minutes; cool 10 minutes.
2 Using hand-held mixer, process soup in pan until smooth. Add remaining stock and beans; stir over medium heat until hot.

tip This thick, creamy soup just begs to be mopped up with a warm, buttered bread roll.

spiced squash and coconut soup

tip For a nice twist, serve chilled or at room temperature in summer, followed by a simple salad.

tomato and bell pepper soup

roasted tomato soup

24 large tomatoes (about 10 pounds), coarsely chopped

6 large red bell peppers, coarsely chopped

3 small onions, coarsely chopped

6 cloves garlic, thinly sliced

prep + cook time 45 minutes
serves 6

1 Preheat oven to 350°F (325°F convection).
2 Combine tomato, bell peppers, onion and garlic in large baking dish; roast, covered, about 30 minutes or until vegetables soften.
3 Push vegetables through food mill or fine sieve into small saucepan; discard solids.
4 Reheat soup.

Serve sprinkled with finely shredded fresh basil, if desired.

creamy white bean soup

2 cans (15 ounces) white beans, rinsed, drained

3 cloves garlic, crushed

2 sprigs fresh thyme

1 cup heavy cream

prep + cook time 30 minutes
serves 4

1 Combine beans, garlic, half the thyme and 4 cups water in large saucepan; bring to a boil. Reduce heat; simmer, uncovered, 25 minutes or until beans are tender. Remove from heat; cool 5 minutes.
2 Discard thyme. Using hand-held blender, process soup in pan until smooth. Add cream; stir over medium heat until hot. Serve sprinkled with thyme leaves from remaining sprigs.

cream of cauliflower soup

1 small cauliflower, broken into florets
1 onion, coarsely chopped
2 cups vegetable stock
½ cup heavy cream

prep + cook time 25 minutes (+ cooling)
serves 6

1 Cook cauliflower and onion in heated oiled large saucepan, stirring, 10 minutes. Add stock and 2 cups of water; bring to a boil. Reduce heat; simmer, covered, about 10 minutes or until cauliflower is soft. Cool 15 minutes.
2 Blend or process soup, in batches, until smooth. Return soup to same pan; stir over medium heat until hot.
3 Drizzle soup with cream.

creamy chickpea and garlic soup

2 cans (15 ounces) chickpeas, rinsed, drained
4 cloves garlic, crushed
2 sprigs fresh rosemary
1¼ cups light cream

prep + cook time 30 minutes
serves 4

1 Combine chickpeas, garlic, half the rosemary and 4 cups water in large saucepan; bring to a boil. Reduce heat; simmer, uncovered, 25 minutes or until chickpeas are tender. Remove from heat; cool 5 minutes.
2 Discard rosemary. Using hand-held blender, process soup in pan until smooth. Add cream; stir over medium heat until hot. Serve sprinkled with rosemary leaves from remaining sprig.

potato and bacon soup

3/4 pound center cut bacon,
   coarsely chopped
2 pounds potatoes, coarsely
   chopped
1 cup chicken stock
1 1/4 cups sour cream

prep + cook time 15 minutes
serves 6

1 Cook bacon, stirring, in heated oiled large
   saucepan until bacon is crisp.
2 Add potato, stock and 2 cups water; bring to a
   boil. Reduce heat; simmer, covered, until potato
   is just tender. Add sour cream; stir until heated
   through (do not boil). Remove from heat; stir in
   some finely chopped parsley, if desired.

italian seafood stew

1 jar (24 ounces) prepared
   marinara sauce
1/2 cup dry white wine
2 pounds frozen seafood mix,
   thawed
1/4 cup finely shredded
   fresh basil

prep + cook time 25 minutes
serves 4

1 Combine marinara sauce, wine and 1 cup
   water in large saucepan; bring to a boil.
   Reduce heat; simmer, uncovered, 10 minutes.
2 Add seafood to pan; cook, covered, stirring
   occasionally, about 5 minutes or until seafood
   just changes color. Stir in basil.

*Use a pasta sauce that has roasted garlic and
herbs to add extra flavor.*

potato and bacon soup

italian seafood stew

tip Idaho potatoes, also known as russets, are commonly available and ideal for this recipe. They have a floury texture and they are excellent for baking, roasting and mashing.

tip Frozen seafood mix, sometimes labeled 'ciopinno', is a combination of uncooked, chopped seafood, typically containing shrimp, salmon, calamari, mussels and scallops.

thai shrimp and squash soup

2 pounds uncooked medium shrimp
¼ cup Thai red curry paste
1 container (32 ounces) creamy butternut squash soup
2 cans (13.75 ounces) light coconut milk

prep + cook time 30 minutes
serves 4

1 Peel and devein shrimp.
2 Stir paste in heated large saucepan until fragrant. Add soup, coconut milk and 1½ cups water to the pan; bring to a boil.
3 Stir in shrimp; reduce heat. Simmer until shrimp are pink.

Serve soup topped with thinly sliced scallion, if desired.

chicken and miso soup

1¼ pounds boneless, skinless chicken thighs, thinly sliced
⅓ cup miso paste
½ pound baby spinach
2 fresh long red chilies, thinly sliced

prep + cook time 15 minutes
serves 6

1 Combine chicken and 6 cups of water in large saucepan; bring to a boil. Reduce heat and cook chicken until white and cooked through.
2 Add miso paste and stir until paste dissolves.
3 Stir in spinach and chiles; serve immediately.

chicken and risoni soup

4 cups chicken stock

3/4 pound boneless skinless chicken breast

2/3 cup risoni pasta

2 tablespoons chopped fresh flat-leaf parsley

prep + cook time 30 minutes
serves 4

1 Bring stock and 3 cups water to a boil in large saucepan; add chicken. Reduce heat; simmer, covered, about 15 minutes or until chicken is cooked through.

2 Remove chicken from stock; reserve stock. Shred chicken coarsely.

3 Add risoni to stock; boil until tender. Return chicken to pan; stir until heated through. Serve soup sprinkled with parsley.

chorizo and lentil soup

2 chorizo sausages (5 ounces each), finely chopped

2 cans (15 ounces) tomato and vegetable soup

1 can (15 ounces) lentil soup

1/3 cup coarsely chopped fresh cilantro

prep + cook time 15 minutes
serves 4

1 Cook chorizo in heated oiled large saucepan, stirring, until crisp; drain excess oil.

2 Add soups to pan; bring to a boil. Reduce heat; simmer, uncovered, 2 minutes. Stir in cilantro before serving.

green salad with cranberries and almonds

10 ounces mixed salad greens
½ cup sliced almonds
½ cup dried cranberries
⅓ cup cranberry and raspberry vinaigrette *(see page 111)*

prep time 15 minutes
serves 8

1 Toast almonds in small dry skillet over medium-high heat until fragrant.
2 Sprinkle salad greens with nuts and cranberries; drizzle with vinaigrette to serve.

Instead of making the vinaigrette, buy one from the supermarket, or use your favorite vinaigrette.

avocado and artichoke salad

4 avocados, sliced
16 jarred artichoke hearts packed in oil, drained, quartered
⅔ cup Italian dressing (see page 110)
2 small heads Boston lettuce, torn

prep time 15 minutes
serves 8

1 Combine avocado, artichoke and dressing in medium bowl; gently toss to coat.
2 Place lettuce in bowl. Serve avocado mixture over lettuce.

beet and goat cheese salad

2 cans (15 ounces) whole baby beets, drained, halved

5 ounces mixed salad greens

2 cups firmly packed fresh mint

1 pound marinated goat cheese in oil

1 Divide combined beets, greens and mint among serving bowls.

2 Drain cheese, reserving 2 tablespoons of oil. Crumble cheese, divide among serving bowls. Serve salad drizzled with reserved oil.

prep time 10 minutes
serves 8

teriyaki beef and radish salad

1/4 cup teriyaki sauce

1 pound beef sirloin

5 ounces baby mesclun

2 red radishes, thinly sliced

1 Combine teriyaki sauce and beef in medium bowl; refrigerate 10 minutes. Drain.

2 Cook drained beef on oiled grill pan until cooked as desired. Cover, stand 5 minutes; slice beef thinly.

3 Combine beef, mesclun and radish in large bowl.

prep + cook time 25 minutes
serves 4

warm smoked salmon salad

1½ pounds baby new potatoes, quartered

5 ounces baby spinach

¾ pound sliced smoked salmon, coarsely chopped

¾ cup creamy dill dressing

1 Boil, steam or microwave potato until tender; drain. Cover to keep warm.

2 Place warm potatoes in large bowl; season. Add spinach and salmon; stir gently.

3 Divide salad among serving plates; drizzle with dressing.

prep + cook time 15 minutes
serves 4

potato, fennel and caper salad

2 pounds potatoes, coarsely chopped

1 large fennel bulb

2 tablespoons rinsed, drained baby capers

⅓ cup honey-mustard dressing (page 108)

1 Boil, steam or microwave potato until tender; drain. Cover to keep warm.

2 Meanwhile, remove fronds from fennel; chop fronds coarsely. Thinly slice fennel bulb.

3 Heat oiled large skillet; cook fennel, stirring, until tender. Place fennel in large bowl with potato, fennel fronds and capers.

4 Add dressing to salad; mix gently. Serve the salad warm.

prep + cook time 15 minutes
serves 6

tip You can use coarsely chopped large potatoes in this salad if you prefer but the baby new potatoes have a fine skin, which you don't need to peel.

warm smoked salmon salad

tip It's always a good idea to rinse capers before using them as they are very salty and their brine has a strong flavor which can overpower the other ingredients in the recipe.

potato, fennel and caper salad

prosciutto, fig and spinach salad

12 large fresh figs (about 2 pounds), quartered

5 ounces baby spinach

1/3 pound thinly sliced prosciutto, torn

1/2 cup balsamic dressing

1 Place figs, spinach, prosciutto and dressing in large bowl; toss gently to combine.

prep time 10 minutes

serves 8

fennel and goat cheese salad

1 cup coarsely chopped walnuts, roasted

6 baby fennel bulbs, trimmed

1/2 cup French dressing

6 ounces fresh goat cheese, crumbled

1 Toast walnuts in a small dry skillet until fragrant.

2 Slice fennel as thinly as possible (use a V-slicer or mandoline, if you can).

3 Combine fennel, nuts and dressing in large bowl. Divide salad among serving plates; sprinkle with cheese.

prep time 30 minutes

serves 4

warm balsamic mushroom salad

1 cup balsamic and garlic
  dressing (page 110)
2 pounds small cremini
  mushrooms
5 ounces mixed salad greens
5 ounces feta cheese, crumbled

1 Heat dressing and $2/3$ cup water in large deep
  skillet; add mushrooms and cook, stirring,
  until mushrooms are tender and liquid has
  almost evaporated. Season to taste.
2 Combine mushrooms and salad leaves in large
  bowl; toss gently. Serve topped with cheese.

prep + cook time 10 minutes
serves 8

summer squash salad

2 pounds mixed patty-pan
  squash, halved
3/4 pound baby new potatoes,
  halved
1/2 cup Italian dressing
  (see page 110)
1 pint cherry tomatoes, halved

1 Boil, steam or microwave squash and
  potatoes, separately, until tender; drain.
2 Combine warm squash and potatoes with
  remaining ingredients in large bowl.

*We used yellow and green patty-pan squash,
just the one variety can be used if you prefer.
Instead of making the dressing, buy one from the
supermarket, or use your favorite dressing.*

prep + cook time 30 minutes
serves 4

potato, prosciutto and pomegranate salad

10 fingerling potatoes (about
   1 pound), halved lengthways
6 slices prosciutto (3 ounces)
4 cups baby spinach
½ cup pomegranate seeds

prep + cook time 20 minutes
serves 4

1 Cook potato in saucepan of boiling water
  10 minutes or until just tender; drain. Cool,
  peel; cut into ½-inch pieces.
2 Preheat broiler, cook prosciutto about 5
  minutes or until crisp; chop coarsely.
3 Combine spinach, potato, prosciutto and
  seeds in large bowl.

*You need to buy a medium pomegranate to
get ½ cup seeds. To remove the seeds, cut
pomegranate in half, then hit the back of the
fruit with a wooden spoon—the seeds usually
fall out easily. Discard the shell and white pith.*

beet and feta salad

1 can (15 ounces) whole baby
  beets, drained, halved
5 ounces mesclun salad mix
1 cup firmly packed fresh mint
1 jar (8 ounces) marinated feta
  in oil

prep time 10 minutes
serves 4

1 Divide combined beets, mesclun and mint
  among serving bowls.
2 Drain feta, reserving 2 tablespoons of oil.
  Chop feta into cubes, divide among serving
  bowls. Serve salad drizzled with reserved oil.

tip Pomegranate is a dark, leathery-skinned fruit about the size of a large orange. Like passionfruit, once you cut through the tough outer skin, the inside is made up of hundreds of seeds. The pulp has a unique tangy sweet-sour flavor and the seeds give it a good crunch.

potato, prosciutto and pomegranate salad

tip Mesclun is a commercial blend of green salad leaves, including baby spinach leaves, curly endive and baby romaine.

beet and feta salad

spinach, bacon and poached egg salad

4 eggs
1 pound center-cut bacon
6 cups baby spinach
⅓ cup Italian dressing
(see page 110)

prep + cook time 20 minutes
serves 4

1 Half fill a large skillet with water; bring to the boil. Break eggs into the pan; return water just to the boil. Cover pan, turn off heat; stand about 4 minutes or until a light film of white sets over each yolk. Using a slotted spoon, remove eggs from pan; rest spoon on paper towel-lined saucer to blot up poaching liquid.
2 Cook bacon in heated oiled large skillet until crisp; drain on paper towel. Chop coarsely.
3 Combine spinach, dressing and bacon in large bowl. Serve salad topped with poached eggs.

parmesan and baby spinach salad

6 cups baby spinach
½ shaved Parmesan cheese
1 tablespoon pine nuts
¼ cup balsamic and garlic dressing *(see page 110)*

prep time 15 minutes
serves 4

1 Toast pine nuts in a small dry skillet over medium-high heat until fragrant.
2 Place spinach, cheese and nuts in large bowl. Add dressing; toss to combine.

Instead of making the dressing, buy one from the supermarket, or use your favorite dressing.

tip This salad is delicious when the egg yolk pours over the other ingredients, mixing with and adding richness to the Italian dressing.

spinach, bacon and poached egg salad

tip This simple salad is the perfect accompaniment to meat or pasta dishes. You could also use arugula, or a mixture of rocket and spinach, if you preferred.

parmesan and baby spinach salad

shrimp and mango salad

2 pounds cooked large shrimp
1 mango, thinly sliced
2 heads baby romaine lettuce, leaves separated
⅓ cup Italian dressing

1 Shell and devein shrimp, leaving tails intact.
2 Combine shrimp and remaining ingredients in large bowl; season to taste.

prep time 25 minutes
serves 4

grilled vegetable salad

¾ pound bottled char-grilled antipasto vegetables, drained, chopped
1 can (15 ounces) chickpeas, rinsed, drained
4 cups mixed salad greens
1 cup tzatziki

1 Combine antipasto, chickpeas and salad leaves in large bowl; toss gently.
2 Serve salad drizzled with tzatziki.

prep time 10 minutes
serves 4

tips To save time, buy shelled shrimp. Serve the salad sprinkled with some chopped chives or parsley if you want a little extra color on your plate.

shrimp and mango salad

tip The delicious mix of grilled vegetables used in antipasto (peppers, eggplant, zucchini and mushroom) as well as the classic combination of brined vegetables, is easy to find in the olive and salad bar sections of most grocery stores. Choose your own combination of favorites to make your signature salad. Ready-made tzatziki is available from the refrigerated dip section of large supermarkets.

grilled vegetable salad

classic caprese salad

6 large roma tomatoes,
  thinly sliced
1 pounds bocconcini cheese,
  drained, thinly sliced
⅓ cup extra virgin olive oil
½ cup firmly packed fresh basil,
  torn

1 Overlap slices of tomato and cheese on
   serving platter.
2 Drizzle with oil; sprinkle with basil.

prep time 15 minutes
serves 4

mixed tomato caprese salad

2 pounds small mixed variety
  tomatoes, thinly sliced
8 ounces bocconcini cheese,
  thinly sliced
⅓ cup coarsely chopped fresh
  basil
¼ cup balsamic and garlic
  dressing *(see page 110)*

1 Layer tomato, cheese and basil on serving plate;
   drizzle with balsamic dressing.

*Instead of making the dressing, buy one from the
supermarket, or use your favorite dressing.*

prep time 20 minutes
serves 4

classic caprese salad

tip This simple salad is native to Campania, the largely agricultural region of Italy that's also home to "mozzarella di bufala", the fresh, stretched, buffalo milk cheese that's a key component of this classic salad. Buffalo mozzarella can be hard to find and expensive, so we used bocconcini instead.

mixed tomato caprese salad

tip We used green and vine-ripened tomatoes. For an extra indulgence, use buffalo-milk mozzarella instead of bocconcini.

mixed cabbage coleslaw

6 cups shredded mixed
  cabbage
1 carrot, coarsely grated
4 scallions, thinly sliced
1/3 cup Asian dressing
  (see page 110)

prep time 20 minutes
serves 4

1 Combine cabbage, carrot and onion in large
  bowl. Add dressing; toss to combine.

*Instead of making the dressing, buy one from the
supermarket, or use your favorite dressing.*

smoked trout and brie salad

1½ pounds firmly packed
  trimmed watercress
3/4 pound smoked trout, flaked
  coarsely
7 ounces brie cheese,
  thinly sliced
1/2 cup mustard dressing

prep time 10 minutes
serves 8

1 Divide watercress, chicken and cheese among
  serving plates; drizzle over dressing.

mixed cabbage coleslaw

tip We used green
and red cabbage
along with some
nappa cabbage in this
coleslaw. For even
faster preparation, try
using pre-shredded
coleslaw mix instead.

smoked trout and brie salad

tip Watercress has
deep green, clover-
shaped leaves that
have a peppery, spicy
flavor. It is highly
perishable and should
be used the day it is
bought.

tuna and cannellini bean salad

2 cups dried cannellini beans
1 can (12 ounces) tuna in
   springwater, drained
1 small red onion, thinly sliced
2 stalks celery, trimmed,
   thinly sliced

prep + cook time 1 hour 10 minutes
(plus standing time)
serves 4

1 Place beans in medium bowl, cover with cold
   water; stand overnight, drain. Rinse under
   cold water; drain.
2 Place beans in medium saucepan of boiling
   water; return to a boil. Reduce heat; simmer,
   uncovered, about 1 hour or until beans are
   almost tender. Drain.
3 Combine beans in large serving bowl with
   tuna, onion and celery. Toss salad with an
   Italian dressing, if desired.

deli pasta salad

1 pound large spiral pasta
1 pound mixed antipasto
   vegetables
2 tablespoons lemon juice
¼ pound sliced salami, cut into
   strips

prep + cook time 20 minutes
serves 6

1 Cook pasta in large saucepan of boiling water
   until tender; drain. Rinse under cold water;
   drain.
2 Meanwhile, drain vegetables, reserving ⅓ cup
   of oil. Combine oil and juice in small bowl;
   season to taste. Coarsely chop vegetables.
3 Combine pasta, vegetables, salami and dressing
   in large bowl; toss gently.

*We used a mix of char-grilled eggplant, bell
peppers, and sundried tomatoes. They are
available in the olive and salad bar section
of most supermarkets.*
Serve sprinkled with shredded basil, if desired.

soba salad with asian greens

6 ounces soba noodles

1/3 cup asian dressing
(see page 110)

2 mandarin oranges,
segmented, coarsely chopped

4 cups tatsoi leaves or
baby bok choy

prep + cook time 20 minutes
serves 4

1 Cook noodles in medium saucepan of boiling
water, uncovered, until tender; drain. Rinse
under cold water; drain.

2 Place noodles and dressing in large bowl with
remaining ingredients; toss gently.

*Instead of making the dressing, buy one from the
supermarket, or use your favorite dressing.
Tatsoi, is a slightly tougher version of bok choy
that was developed to grow close to the ground
so it is easily protected from frost. If tatsoi is
unavailable, use bok choy instead.*

warm gnocchi salad

2/3 cup roasted walnuts

3 jars (10 ounces) marinated
artichoke hearts packed in
olive oil

2 pounds fresh potato gnocchi

1 cup black olives

prep + cook time 20 minutes
serves 8

1 Toast walnuts in a small dry skillet over
medium-high heat until fragrant.

2 Drain artichokes, reserving 1/2 cup oil; quarter
artichokes.

3 Cook gnocchi in large saucepan of boiling
water until gnocchi float to the surface; drain.

4 Combine olives, artichoke, reserved oil and
gnocchi in large bowl; toss gently. Sprinkle
with nuts.

Serve sprinkled with shredded basil, if desired.

lemon and macadamia dressing

1 lemon
½ cup macadamia oil
⅓ cup macadamia nuts
1 teaspoon sugar

prep time 10 minutes
makes 1 cup

1 Toast nuts in a small dry skillet over medium-high heat until fragrant. Let cool; chop finely.
2 Grate zest from lemon (you need 1 teaspoon); juice lemon (you need ¼ cup).
3 Whisk zest, juice and remaining ingredients in small bowl until combined.

honey mustard dressing

½ cup mayonnaise
¼ cup cider vinegar
1 tablespoon honey
2 teaspoons wholegrain mustard

prep time 5 minutes
makes 1 cup

1 Whisk ingredients in small jug until combined.

tip Macadamia oil has a mild, unobtrusive nutty flavor that works well with seafood salads, or other delicate salads that shouldn't be overpowered by olive oil.

lemon and macadamia dressing

tip This classic salad dressing is creamy and sweet with a sharp tang given by the cider vinegar.

honey mustard dressing

balsamic and garlic dressing

¼ cup balsamic vinegar

2 tablespoons lemon juice

2 cloves garlic, crushed

¾ cup olive oil

1 Whisk ingredients in small bowl until smooth.

prep time 10 minutes
makes 1¼ cup

italian dressing

⅔ cup olive oil

⅓ cup white wine vinegar

1 clove garlic, crushed

2 tablespoons finely chopped mixed fresh herbs

1 Combine ingredients in screw-top jar; shake well.

We used oregano and basil, use whatever fresh herbs you like.

prep time 5 minutes
makes 1 cup

asian dressing

⅓ cup lime juice

2 fresh long red chiles, thinly sliced

1 piece (2 inches) fresh ginger, peeled and cut into matchsticks

¼ cup peanut oil

1 Whisk ingredients in small bowl until smooth.

prep time 10 minutes
makes ⅔ cup

blue cheese dressing

⅓ cup buttermilk

3 ounces blue cheese, crumbled

1 tablespoon lemon juice

1 tablespoon finely chopped garlic chives

1 Whisk ingredients in small bowl until smooth.

prep time 10 minutes

makes ⅔ cup

creamy dill dressing

½ cup sour cream

¼ cup lemon juice

2 tablespoons finely chopped fresh dill

1 Whisk sour cream, juice and 1 tablespoon hot water in small bowl. Stir in dill.

prep time 10 minutes

makes ¾ cup

cranberry and raspberry vinaigrette

¼ cup red wine vinegar

½ cup olive oil

½ cup fresh raspberries

¼ cup whole-berry cranberry sauce

1 Blend or process ingredients until smooth. Push through fine sieve into small bowl. Discard solids.

Use raspberry vinegar in place of red wine vinegar for an extra fruity taste. If the dressing is too thick, stir in a little cold water.

prep time 15 minutes

makes 1 cup

Vegetarian

Whether you're craving a heart-warming casserole, a garden-fresh pasta creation or a super-fast stir fry, there are plenty of main dishes that don't require meat as the main attraction.

34

bruschetta caprese

½ long loaf turkish bread or
   focaccia

1 pint cherry tomatoes,
   thickly sliced

4 ounces baby bocconcini
   cheese, thickly sliced

1 cup loosely packed fresh basil

prep + cook time 15 minutes
serves 4

1 Preheat broiler.
2 Cut bread crossways into four even pieces;
   split each piece horizontally. Toast bread,
   cut-sides up, under broiler.
3 Place two slices toast on each serving plate.
   Top with tomato, cheese and basil; drizzle with
   extra virgin olive oil, if desired.

roasted cherry tomatoes, feta and avocado on turkish bread

1 pint cherry tomatoes, halved

½ large loaf turkish bread,
   halved

1 avocado, thinly sliced

4 ounce piece feta cheese,
   crumbled

prep + cook time 15 minutes
serves 4

1 Preheat broiler.
2 Cook tomatoes under broiler about 5 minutes
   or until softened.
3 Meanwhile, split bread pieces horizontally;
   toast cut sides. Top toast with avocado, tomato
   and cheese; broil about 2 minutes or until hot.
   Serve sprinkled with basil, if desired.

bruschetta caprese

tip Layer your ingredients carefully and artfully into a colorful little stack. The baby bocconcini is sold in supermarkets, in tubs of brine or water.

oasted cherry tomatoes, feta and avocado on turkish bread

tip Adding avocado to this open sandwich not only adds a rich creamy flavor, it also increases its nutritional value. Avocados are a rich source of potassium and healthy monounsaturated fats that help to lower cholesterol.

asparagus, egg and hollandaise

1 pound asparagus, trimmed
4 eggs
2/3 cup hollandaise sauce
1/4 cup shaved Parmesan cheese

prep + cook time 35 minutes
serves 4

1 Boil, steam or microwave asparagus until tender; drain.
2 Fill medium deep skillet with water; bring to a gentle simmer. Break one egg into a cup, then slide into pan; repeat with remaining eggs. Cook eggs, uncovered, about 2 minutes or until white is set and yolk is still runny. Remove with slotted spoon; drain on paper towels.
3 Serve asparagus topped with eggs, hollandaise and cheese.

Serve sprinkled with chopped fresh dill, if desired.

spinach and corn pies

2 potatoes, diced into 1/2 inch pieces
1/2 pound frozen spinach, thawed, drained
2 cans (15 ounces) creamed corn
1 1/2 packages (15 ounces) pie dough (enough for 3 crusts)

prep + cook time 1 hour
makes 6

1 Cook potato in heated oiled large skillet, stirring, until browned lightly. Combine potato, spinach and corn in large bowl.
2 Preheat oven to 400°F (375°F convection). Coat a baking sheet with cooking spray.
3 Cut each crust in half. Place equal amounts of filling on one half of each portion; fold pastry in half to enclose filling, press edges with fork to seal.
4 Place pies on sheet; coat with cooking spray. Bake about 30 minutes or until lightly browned. Serve with sweet chili sauce, if desired.

asparagus, egg and hollandaise

tip You can add 1 tablespoon of white vinegar to the simmering water before adding the eggs in step 2. The acid helps to set the egg whites.

spinach and corn pies

tip Originating from Cornwall in the United Kingdom, these savory pies, known as 'pasties' in England, were devised as a hearty meal for Cornish tin miners who couldn't come to the surface to eat. The traditional semi-circular shaped Cornish pasties were filled with diced meat, sliced potato and onion. Sometimes a sweet filling was added to one end of the pastie, making it a combined lunch and dessert meal in one.

tortilla de patata

⅓ cup olive oil

3 potatoes (about 1 pound),
   finely chopped

1 onion, finely chopped

8 eggs, lightly beaten

prep + cook time 40 minutes
serves 4

1 Preheat oven to 350°F (325°F convection).
2 Heat oil in 9-inch ovenproof skillet; cook
   potato and onion, covered, stirring
   occasionally, until potato is tender.
3 Add eggs to pan. Cook, uncovered, over low
   heat, about 5 minutes or until egg is just set.
4 Place pan in oven; cook, uncovered, about
   10 minutes or until lightly browned. Carefully
   turn tortilla onto large plate. Cut into wedges;
   serve with a side salad, if desired.

blue cheese baked potatoes

4 large potatoes, unpeeled

¾ cup sour cream

2 ounces blue cheese,
   crumbled

prep + cook time 1 hour 10 minutes
makes 4

1 Preheat oven to 350°F (325°F convection).
2 Pierce potatoes with fork; wrap in foil. Bake
   potatoes about 1 hour.
3 Meanwhile, combine sour cream and cheese
   in small bowl.
4 Cut cross in potatoes; squeeze with tongs
   to open. Divide sour cream mixture among
   potatoes. Sprinkle with crumbled bacon,
   if a non-vegetarian dish is desired.

tortilla de patata

tip This is a classic Spanish tortilla but you can try adding other ingredients from your pantry: a pinch of dried red pepper flakes, frozen peas, sun-dried tomatoes or roasted bell pepper for instance.

blue cheese baked potatoes

tips Don't be put off by eating the potato skins. They are an excellent source of fiber and vitamin B6. Scrub the potatoes well under water just before use.

bean and tomato quesadillas

8 large flour tortillas)
1 can (15 ounces) refried beans
2 tomatoes, finely chopped
2 cups coarsely grated Cheddar
  cheese

prep + cook time 20 minutes
serves 4

1 Place one tortilla on work surface; spread with a quarter of the beans. Sprinkle with a quarter of the tomato and cheese. Top with second tortilla. Repeat with remaining tortillas, beans, tomato and cheese to make four quesadillas.
2 Cook quesadillas, one at a time, in heated oiled large skillet, over medium heat, until browned lightly both sides. Cut into wedges; serve with sour cream, if desired.

red curry lentils

2 tablespoons red curry paste
1 cup dried brown lentils,
  rinsed, drained
2 cups baby spinach
2 tablespoons lime juice

prep + cook time 40 minutes
serves 4

1 Cook curry paste in medium saucepan, stirring, until fragrant. Add lentils and 2 cups water; bring to a boil. Reduce heat; simmer, uncovered, about 10 minutes or until lentils are tender.
2 Add spinach to pan; cook until just wilted. Remove from heat; stir in juice.
3 Divide curry among serving bowls.

Serve with yogurt.

tomato, leek and feta tarts

6 ounces marinated feta
  cheese

1 leek

2 sheets puff pastry, frozen,
  thawed

1 pint cherry tomatoes,
  thinly sliced

prep + cook time 50 minutes
serves 4

1 Preheat oven to 425°F (400°F convection).

2 Drain marinated feta; reserve 1 tablespoon
  of the oil.

3 Cut leek into 3-inch pieces; cut pieces in half
  lengthways, slice halves lengthways into thin
  strips. Heat reserved oil in large skillet; cook
  leek, stirring occasionally, about 20 minutes
  or until soft.

4 Meanwhile, cut each pastry sheet into four
  squares; place on lightly oiled oven trays. Fold
  edges of pastry over to make a 1/4-inch border
  around pastry; prick pastry pieces with fork.
  Bake, uncovered, in oven, about 10 minutes or
  until lightly browned. Remove from oven;
  using fork, immediately press pastry pieces
  down to flatten. Reduce oven temperature to
  400°F (375°F convection).

5 Divide the leek mixture and place equal
  amounts over each pastry piece; crumble
  cheese over each then top with tomato. Bake,
  uncovered, about 5 minutes or until tomato
  just softens. Serve immediately.

tip To make your own marinated
feta, cut 6 ounces feta cheese into
1/2-inch pieces. Combine 2 teaspoons
finely grated lemon zest, 2 tablespoons
finely chopped fresh oregano and
1 cup chile-infused olive oil in small
bowl. Place cheese in sterilized jar;
pour over oil mixture. Refrigerate 3
hours or overnight. Store any unused
marinated feta in the refrigerator.

caramelized fennel tarts

3 oranges

8 baby fennel bulbs, trimmed, halved lengthways

2 sheets frozen puff pastry, thawed

1 tablespoon finely chopped fresh thyme

prep + cook time 45 minutes
makes 4

1 Preheat oven to 425°F (400°F convection).

2 Finely grate 1 orange (you need 2 teaspoons zest); juice oranges (you need 1 cup juice).

3 Heat oiled large skillet; cook fennel until browned lightly. Add zest and juice; bring to a boil. Reduce heat; simmer, uncovered, about 5 minutes or until fennel is caramelized and tender.

4 Cut each pastry sheet into four squares; place on baking sheet lined with parchment paper. Remove fennel from skillet, leaving pan juices; divide among pastry squares. Bake about 20 minutes or until pastry is browned.

5 Meanwhile, return pan juices to a boil. Reduce heat; simmer, uncovered, until sauce thickens slightly. Serve tarts drizzled with sauce and sprinkled with thyme.

spinach and beet tarts

2 sheets frozen puff pasty, thawed

1 pound frozen spinach, thawed, drained

12 ounces feta cheese, crumbled

2 cans (15 ounces) baby beets, drained, thinly sliced

prep + cook time 30 minutes
serves 4

1 Preheat oven to 425°F (400°F convection). Line baking sheets with parchment paper.

2 Arrange pastry on sheet. Fold edges over to make a ¼-inch border all the way around pastry. Prick pastry base with fork. Place another lightly oiled baking sheet on top of pastry; bake 10 minutes. Remove top tray from pastry; reduce temperature to 400°F (375°F convection).

3 Meanwhile, combine spinach with half the cheese in medium bowl.

4 Top tarts with spinach mixture, beets and remaining cheese. Bake about 10 minutes or until heated through.

caramelized fennel tarts

spinach and beet tarts

tip Try sprinkling the tarts with crumbled goat cheese 5 minutes before the end of baking time.

tip Drain the spinach really well so that the moisture does not seep into the tart base and make the pastry soggy.

wild mushroom risotto

4 cups vegetable stock

1 pound mixed mushrooms, chopped

2 cups arborio rice

½ cup finely grated Parmesan cheese

prep + cook time 35 minutes
serves 4

1 Bring stock and 2 cups water to a boil in medium saucepan. Reduce heat; simmer, covered.

2 Meanwhile, cook mushrooms in oiled large saucepan, stirring, until just tender and any liquid evaporates; remove from pan.

3 Add rice to same pan; cook, stirring, 1 minute. Return mushrooms to pan. Add 1 cup simmering stock mixture; cook, stirring, over low heat, until stock is absorbed. Continue adding stock mixture, in 1-cup batches, stirring, until absorbed between additions. Total cooking time should be about 25 minutes or until rice is tender. Stir in cheese.

We used chestnut, button, flat, chanterelle and porcini mushrooms; use any combination of mushrooms you like.
Serve with fresh crusty bread.

vegetable curry

2 tablespoons yellow curry paste

1 pound butternut squash, peeled and coarsely chopped

½ small cauliflower, cut into florets

1 cup Greek-style yogurt

prep + cook time 35 minutes
serves 4

1 Cook curry paste in heated oiled large saucepan until fragrant. Add butternut squash; cook, stirring, 2 minutes. Add 1½ cups water; bring to a boil. Reduce heat; simmer, uncovered, 5 minutes.

2 Add cauliflower; simmer, uncovered, 10 minutes or until vegetables are just tender. Add yogurt; stir over low heat until hot. Serve with steamed rice and lemon wedges, if desired.

slow-roasted mushrooms

1½ pounds mixed mushrooms, coarsely chopped

¾ pound vine-ripened tomatoes, coarsely chopped

1 small red onion, thinly sliced

1 tablespoon olive oil

prep + cook time 50 minutes
serves 4

1 Preheat oven to 325°F (300°F convection).
2 Combine ingredients in large baking dish; roast, uncovered, about 40 minutes or until mushrooms are tender.
3 If you like, serve the mushrooms with soft polenta and sprinkle with chopped chives.

We used oyster, shiitake, swiss brown and flat mushrooms for this recipe.

cheesy polenta

2⅓ cups milk

1 cup polenta

½ cup grated Parmesan cheese

2 tablespoons butter

prep + cook time 20 minutes
serves 4

1 Combine milk with 2⅓ cups water in large saucepan; bring to a boil. Gradually add polenta to liquid, stirring constantly. Reduce heat; simmer, stirring, about 10 minutes or until polenta thickens. Stir in cheese and butter.

mushroom and spinach gnocchi

1¼ pounds fresh potato gnocchi
¾ pound assorted mushrooms, thinly sliced
1 cups heavy cream
3 cups baby spinach

prep + cook time 10 minutes
serves 4

1 Cook gnocchi in large pot of boiling water until gnocchi float to the surface; drain.
2 Meanwhile, cook mushrooms in heated oiled large skillet, stirring, until softened. Add cream and spinach; bring to the boil. Reduce heat, simmer, uncovered, until spinach wilts and sauce thickens. Season to taste.
3 Add gnocchi to skillet, stir gently.

Serve sprinkled with grated Parmesan cheese, if desired.

gnocchi formaggio

1 pound potato gnocchi
1 cup light cream
2 ounces gorgonzola cheese, crumbled coarsely
1 cup coarsely grated pecorino cheese

prep + cook time 20 minutes
serves 4

1 Cook gnocchi in large pot of boiling water until gnocchi float to the surface; drain.
2 Meanwhile, bring cream to a boil in small saucepan. Reduce heat; simmer, uncovered, 3 minutes or until reduced by half.
3 Remove cream from heat; gradually stir in cheeses until smooth.
4 Return gnocchi to pot with cheese sauce; stir gently to combine.

Serve with chopped chives or baby arugula if desired.

mushroom and spinach gnocchi

tip We used a mixture of white button and portobello mushrooms for this recipe.

gnocchi formaggio

tip Gnocchi are Italian 'dumplings' that are most commonly made from potatoes or semolina. They can be found in most supermarkets and Italian grocery stores.

spaghetti with pesto

¾ pound spaghetti

¼ cup bottled basil pesto

2 tablespoons lemon juice

¼ cup coarsely grated
Parmesan cheese

prep + cook time 35 minutes
serves 4

1 Cook pasta in large pot of boiling water until
tender; drain.

2 Return pasta to pot; add pesto, juice and
cheese. Toss to combine.

broccoli and garlic breadcrumb spaghetti

12 slices stale white bread

1 pound spaghetti

½ pound broccoli crowns,
cut into florets

2 cloves garlic, crushed

prep + cook time 25 minutes
serves 4

1 Remove and discard crusts from bread; process
bread until fine.

2 Cook pasta in large pot of boiling water until
tender; drain.

3 Meanwhile, boil, steam or microwave broccoli
until tender; drain.

4 Cook breadcrumbs and garlic in oiled large
skillet until lightly browned and crisp.

5 Combine pasta, broccoli and breadcrumbs in
a large bowl.

fettuccine alfredo

1½ pounds fresh fettuccine
    pasta
8 tablespoons (1 stick) butter
1¾ cups heavy cream
¾ cup grated Parmesan cheese

prep + cook time 30 minutes
serves 6

1 Cook pasta in large pot of boiling water until tender; drain. Return to pan.
2 Meanwhile, melt butter in medium skillet, add cream; bring to a boil. Reduce heat; simmer, uncovered, about 8 minutes or until sauce reduces by half. Stir in cheese, over low heat, about 2 minutes or until cheese melts.
3 Add sauce to pasta; toss gently to coat.

This sauce is named after the Roman restaurateur Alfredo di Lello who created the dish in the 1920s. Do not reduce the cream mixture too rapidly or by too much as this sauce can burn. Check and stir once or twice and take the pan off the heat when it is reduced correctly.

fettuccine with grilled vegetables

2 pounds fettuccine pasta
1½ pounds roasted antipasto
    vegetables in oil
10 ounces baby spinach
2 cups Parmesan cheese

prep + cook time 20 minutes
serves 8

1 Cook pasta in large pot of boiling water until tender; drain.
2 Meanwhile, drain vegetables; reserve ½ cup of the oil. Chop vegetables coarsely. Cook vegetables with reserved oil in large saucepan until heated through.
3 Toss hot pasta with vegetable mixture, spinach and half the cheese. Serve topped with remaining cheese.

Roasted vegetables are often available in the olive and salad bar section of many grocery stores. Choose your favorite combination for a signature dish.

fresh tomato and chile pasta

1½ pounds penne pasta

2 fresh small red Thai chiles, finely chopped

6 ripe tomatoes, coarsely chopped

1½ cups coarsely chopped fresh flat-leaf parsley

prep + cook time 20 minutes
serves 6

1 Cook pasta in large pot of boiling water until tender; drain.

2 Meanwhile, heat oiled large skillet; cook chile, stirring, about 1 minute or until fragrant. Stir in tomato and parsley; remove from heat.

3 Add sauce mixture to pasta; toss gently.

Serve sprinkled with flaked Parmesan cheese.

pasta with roasted tomatoes

16 roma tomatoes, quartered

4 cloves garlic, crushed

½ cup olive oil

2 pounds penne pasta

prep + cook time 30 minutes
serves 8

1 Preheat oven to 425°F (400°F convection).

2 Combine tomato, garlic and oil in large baking dish; roast, uncovered, about 15 minutes or until tomato softens and browns slightly.

3 Meanwhile, cook pasta in large pot of boiling water until tender; drain.

4 Place tomato mixture and pasta in large bowl; toss gently.

Serve sprinkled with small basil leaves.

fresh tomato and chile pasta

pasta with roasted tomatoes

tip This is a great basic pasta sauce; add drained and flaked canned tuna, drained bottled antipasto mix, or slices of salami for quick variations.

tip Roasting fresh tomatoes brings out their sweetness and creates a delicious, light sauce to coat the pasta. Sauce made from fresh tomatoes beats any bottled tomato pasta sauce hands down.

zucchini and ricotta farfalle

1½ pounds farfalle pasta
40 zucchini flowers with stem attached
2 lemons
1¾ cups ricotta cheese, crumbled

prep + cook time 20 minutes
serves 8

1 Cook pasta in large pot of boiling water until tender; drain. Return pasta to pan.
2 Meanwhile, cut stems from zucchini flowers; chop coarsely. Remove and discard stamens from flowers.
3 Finely grate 2 teaspoons zest from lemon. Squeeze juice from lemon (you need ⅔ cup juice).
4 Heat oiled large skillet; cook chopped zucchini stems, stirring, until tender. Add zucchini flowers, zest and juice; cook until wilted.
5 Gently stir zucchini mixture and cheese into pasta. Season to taste.

Serve sprinkled with chives, if desired.

lemon and ricotta-filled zucchini flowers

1 lemon
8 ounces ricotta cheese
2 tablespoons grated Parmesan cheese
12 zucchini flowers with stem attached

prep + cook time 35 minutes
serves 4

1 Grate zest from lemon (you need 1 teaspoon); juice lemon (you need 1 tablespoon). Combine cheeses, zest and juice in small bowl.
2 Discard stamens from inside zucchini flowers; fill flowers with cheese mixture, twist petal tops to enclose filling.
3 Place zucchini flowers, in single layer, in large bamboo steamer, over large saucepan of boiling water. Steam, covered, about 15 minutes or until zucchini are tender.

zucchini and ricotta farfalle

lemon and ricotta-filled zucchini flowers

tips The stems are actually baby zucchini still attached to the flowers. If zucchini flowers are unavailable just use thinly sliced zucchini instead.

tip Zucchini flowers, the prize of summer at many farmers markets, have a subtle zucchini flavor and are usually stuffed with a mild-flavored filling and deep-fried, steamed or baked.

lemon, pea and ricotta pasta

2 lemons
¾ pound angel hair pasta
2 cups frozen peas
¾ cup crumbled ricotta cheese

prep + cook time 15 minutes
serves 4

1 Grate zest from 1 lemon (you need 1 teaspoon). Juice lemons (you need ½ cup).
2 Cook pasta in large pot of boiling water until tender; add peas during last minute of pasta cooking time. Drain, reserving ¼ cup cooking liquid. Rinse pasta and peas under cold water; drain.
3 Combine pasta and peas in large bowl with reserved cooking liquid, zest and juice; stir in cheese.

pasta with pizzaiola sauce

2 cans (15 ounces) crushed tomatoes
2 cloves garlic, crushed
2 tablespoons finely chopped fresh oregano
¾ pound spaghetti

prep + cook time 45 minutes
serves 4

1 Bring undrained tomatoes and garlic to a boil in heated oiled large skillet. Reduce heat; simmer, uncovered, about 25 minutes or until liquid is reduced by half. Stir in oregano.
2 Meanwhile, cook pasta in large pot of boiling water until tender; drain. Remove from heat. Add pasta to sauce; toss pasta to coat in sauce.

fennel and gorgonzola gratins

1½ pounds butternut squash, peeled, thinly sliced

2 baby fennel bulbs with fronds

4 ounces gorgonzola cheese, coarsely crumbled

2 cups light cream

prep + cook time 35 minutes
serves 4

1 Preheat oven to 400°F (375°F convection). Coat four 1-cup shallow dishes. with cooking spray.

2 Boil, steam or microwave butternut squash until tender.

3 Slice fennel thinly; chop fronds finely. Layer fennel, half the fronds, three-quarters of the cheese and the butternut squash in dishes.

4 Heat cream in small saucepan, stirring, until hot; pour into dishes. Cover dishes with foil; bake, in oven, 20 minutes.

5 Preheat broiler.

6 Remove foil from dishes; broil until browned. Serve gratins sprinkled with remaining fennel fronds.

Fennel fronds are the delicate feathery tips of the fennel plant. They have a light aniseed flavor.

butternut squash lasagna

3 fresh lasagna sheets

8 tablespoons (1 stick) butter, coarsely chopped

¾ pound peeled butternut squash, finely chopped

12 fresh sage leaves

prep + cook time 25 minutes
serves 4

1 Cut each lasagne sheet into quarters. Cook pasta, in batches, in large pot of boiling water until tender; drain. Place pasta sheets, in single layer, on tray; cover to keep warm.

2 Meanwhile, heat one-quarter of the butter in large skillet; cook pumpkin, stirring, about 10 minutes or until tender. Season to taste; remove from pan, cover to keep warm.

3 Heat remaining butter in same pan until lightly browned. Add sage; remove from heat.

4 Place one pasta sheet on each of four serving plates. Top with half the pumpkin then another pasta sheet. Repeat with remaining pumpkin and pasta. Drizzle with sage butter.

Seafood

Fish and seafood dishes are marvelous additions to any repertoire because they're so easy to put together with just a few basic ingredients. From spicy baked fish to freshly steamed mussels, these quick and flavorful recipes are just as suitable for a dinner party as they are a quick weeknight meal.

34

fish in macadamia butter

½ cup macadamias

5 tablespoons butter

⅓ cup finely chopped fresh
  cilantro

4 white fish fillets
  (6 ounces each)

prep + cook time 15 minutes
serves 4

1 Toast nuts in large dry skillet over medium-high heat, shaking pan constantly, until fragrant; remove from heat. When cool enough to handle, chop nuts coarsely.

2 Melt butter in same pan; cook nuts and cilantro, stirring, 1 minute. Add fish; cook, turning halfway through cooking time, until cooked through.

3 Drizzle fish with butter. Serve with steamed baby green beans, if desired.

peri peri fish with mixed greens

48 firm white fish fillets

⅓ cup peri peri marinade

4 cups mixed salad greens

1 tablespoon lemon juice

prep + cook time 20 minutes
serves 4

1 Drizzle fish with marinade, coating both sides. Cook fish, in batches, in heated oiled large grill pan until cooked through.

2 Meanwhile, combine greens and juice in medium bowl; season to taste.

3 Serve fish with salad.

fish in macademia butter

tip Macadamia nuts are native to Australia but grown and eaten around the globe. They're little perfect spheres of goodness, with a delicate flavor and a crunchy texture containing a high percentage of the "good" monounsaturated fats.

peri peri fish with mixed greens

tips Peri peri, also spelled piri piri, is a hot chili sauce and marinade used in Portuguese, African and Brazilian cooking. It is available from most major supermarkets and gourmet food stores.

salt and pepper trout

6 ocean rainbow trout fillets
(6 ounces each), skin on

1½ teaspoons peppercorn,
coarsely crushed

1 teaspoon sea salt

½ pound watercress, trimmed

prep + cook time 15 minutes
serves 6

1 Score skin on fish three times; coat skin
with combined pepper and salt. Cook fish,
skin-side down, in heated oiled large skillet,
about 5 minutes or until browned and crisp.
Turn fish; cook about 3 minutes or until
cooked through.

2 Serve fish with watercress.

orange and mustard-glazed fish

½ cup orange juice

2 tablespoons Dijon mustard

1 tablespoon olive oil

8 white fish fillets (6 ounces
each), skin on

prep + cook time 25 minutes
serves 8

1 Preheat oven to 475°F (450°F convection).
Line baking sheet with parchment paper.

2 Combine juice, mustard, oil and fish in
medium bowl.

3 Place fish on sheet; roast about 12 minutes or
until fish is cooked through.

crumbed rainbow trout

2 tablespoons olive oil
2 cups fresh breadcrumbs
2 teaspoons fresh lime zest
8 rainbow trout fillets
(6 ounces each)

prep + cook time 25 minutes
serves 8

1 Preheat oven to 475°F (450°F convection). Line baking sheet with parchment paper.
2 Combine oil, breadcrumbs and zest in medium bowl. Place fish on sheet; pat crumb mixture onto fish. Roast about 12 minutes or until fish is cooked through.

oven-steamed ocean trout

4 rainbow trout fillets
(6 ounces each)
2 tablespoons lemon juice
1 tablespoon rinsed, drained capers, coarsely chopped
2 teaspoons coarsely chopped fresh dill

prep + cook time 25 minutes
serves 4

1 Preheat oven to 400°F (375°F convection).
2 Place each fillet on a square of foil large enough to completely enclose fish; top with equal amounts of juice, capers and dill. Gather corners of foil squares together above fish, twist to close securely.
3 Place foil parcels on baking sheet; cook about 15 minutes or until fish is cooked through. Let stand 5 minutes. Open carefully so steam is directed away from you.
4 Serve fish with boiled potatoes, if desired.

cajun-style fish

2 tablespoons cajun seasoning

2 teaspoons fresh lemon zest

1 tablespoon vegetable oil

4 white fish fillets
  (6 ounces each)

prep + cook time 20 minutes
serves 4

1 Combine seasoning, zest and oil in small bowl. Rub mixture over fish.

2 Cook fish in heated oiled grill pan until cooked through. Serve fish with coleslaw or salad, if desired.

snapper fillets with ginger soy syrup

2 carrots, cut into matchsticks

2 zucchini, cut into matchsticks

4 snapper fillets (8 ounces each), skin on

1 cup bottled sweet chili, ginger and soy marinade

prep + cook time 35 minutes
serves 4

1 Boil, steam or microwave carrot and zucchini, separately, until tender.

2 Meanwhile, score fish skin. Cook fish, skin-side down, in heated oiled large skillet about 5 minutes. Turn fish; cook about 3 minutes until cooked through. Remove from pan.

3 Add 1/3 cup water and marinade to pan; stir until hot.

4 Serve fish with sauce and vegetables.

Serve with steamed jasmine rice.

cajun-style fish

tip We made a very simple warm bean salad to go with this recipe. Cook 1 thinly sliced small red onion and 1 coarsely chopped large tomato in a heated medium saucepan until soft. Add a 15-ounce can of rinsed, drained kidney beans and stir until mixture is heated through.

snapper fillets with ginger soy syrup

tip Julienning is a method of cutting vegetables into long thin strips (also called matchsticks). You can buy 'julienne peelers' that have very sharp teeth, or, alternatively, just cut them very carefully using a sharp knife.

smoked cod with parsley butter

8 smoked cod fillets
(6 ounces each)

4 tablespoons butter, softened

2 tablespoons finely chopped
fresh flat-leaf parsley

prep + cook time 35 minutes
serves 8

1 Place fish in large deep skillet; cover with cold water. Bring slowly to a gentle simmer, uncovered. Remove from heat; drain. Repeat process once more; drain.
2 Combine butter and parsley in small bowl.
3 Preheat broiler.
4 Divide fish among eight 1½-cup shallow ovenproof dishes; dollop with parsley butter. Stand dishes on baking sheets; broil until butter melts.

fish cutlets with pesto butter

4 tablespoons butter, softened

2 tablespoons basil pesto

1 teaspoon fresh lemon zest

4 white fish cutlets
(6 ounces each)

prep + cook time 20 minutes
serves 4

1 Stir butter, pesto and zest in small bowl until well combined.
2 Cook fish in heated oiled large skillet until cooked through. Remove from pan.
3 Place butter mixture in same pan; stir over low heat until butter melts. Return fish to pan; turn to coat in butter mixture. Serve fish on a bed of baby spinach, if desired.

almond crumbed fish

¼ cup finely grated Parmesan
cheese

1 cup ground almond

2 eggs

4 white fish fillets
(8 ounces each)

prep + cook time 35 minutes
serves 4

1 Preheat oven to 450°F (450°F convection).
2 Combine cheese and ground almond in
medium shallow bowl; beat eggs in another
medium shallow bowl.
3 Coat fish all over in egg, then coat in almond
mixture. Place fish, in single layer, on oiled
baking sheet; spray with cooking-oil spray.
Roast fish, uncovered, about 20 minutes or
until cooked through.

fast fish vindaloo

4 white fish fillets (6 ounces
each), skin on

1 large onion, thinly sliced

¼ cup vindaloo curry paste

2 tomatoes, coarsely chopped

prep + cook time 30 minutes
serves 4

1 Cook fish in heated oiled large skillet, skin-side
down, until browned. Turn; cook other side
until browned. Remove from skillet.
2 Cook onion in same skillet, stirring, until onion
softens. Add curry paste; cook, stirring, until
fragrant. Add tomato and 1 cup water; bring
to a boil. Reduce heat; simmer, uncovered,
5 minutes.
3 Return fish to skillet; simmer, uncovered, about
5 minutes or until fish is cooked through. If
desired, sprinkle vindaloo with cilantro and
serve with steamed rice and yogurt.

lemon fish in parchment

1 can (15 ounces) whole peeled baby potatoes, drained, halved
3/4 pound asparagus, trimmed
4 firm white fish fillets (6 ounces each)
1/4 cup lemon juice

prep + cook time 25 minutes
serves 4

1 Preheat oven to 400°F (375°F convection).
2 Place four large squares of parchment paper on top of four large squares of foil; layer potato and asparagus on squares. Top with fish fillets. Drizzle fish with juice; enclose fish in foil.
3 Place parcels on oven tray; bake about 15 minutes until fish is cooked through. Let stand 5 minutes; open carefully so stem is directed away from you.

salmon and spinach in phyllo

1 pounds spinach, trimmed
46 sheets frozen phyllo pastry, thawed
4 salmon fillets (6 ounces each)
2 cups prepared marinara sauce

prep + cook time 40 minutes
serves 4

1 Preheat oven to 425°F (400°F convection). Line baking sheet with parchment paper.
2 Boil, steam or microwave spinach until wilted. Rinse under cold water; drain. Squeeze out excess liquid; coarsely chop.
3 Spray each sheet of pastry with oil. Fold each sheet in half widthways. Place one sheet on work surface; center one salmon fillet on pastry, top with one fourth of the spinach. Fold in sides of pastry and roll to enclose filling. Spray parcel with oil; place on baking sheet, seam-side down. Repeat to make three more parcels.
4 Bake parcels about 15 minutes or until pastry is browned lightly and fish is cooked as desired.
5 Bring sauce to a boil in small saucepan. Serve with parcels.

lemon fish in parchment

tip You can use any firm white fish in this recipe. Snapper and cod are both good choices. Remove any small bones with tweezers.

salmon and spinach in phyllo

tips It's important to squeeze as much liquid from the spinach as possible to prevent the phyllo pastry going soggy. The salmon will be cooked medium, slightly pink in the middle, in this recipe. Increase or decrease the baking time depending on how you like your salmon cooked.

herb and tomato fish bundles

4 firm white fish fillets
   (6 ounces each)
½ pint cherry tomatoes, halved
1 tablespoon baby capers in
   vinegar
4 thyme sprigs

prep + cook time 30 minutes
serves 4

1 Preheat oven to 400°F (375°F convection).
2 Place each fillet on a large square of parchment paper or foil. Drain capers; reserve vinegar. Divide tomato, capers, thyme and reserved caper vinegar among fish pieces. Gather corners of paper or foil together above fish; twist to enclose securely.
3 Place parcels on baking sheet; bake 15 minutes until fish is cooked through. Let stand 5 minutes; open carefully so stem is directed away from you.

mediterranean baked fish

4 whole white fish
   (12 ounces each)
½ cup chopped coarsely
   mixed fresh herbs
2 lemons, thinly sliced
4 tomatoes, chopped coarsely

prep + cook time 35 minutes
serves 4

1 Preheat oven to 400°F (375°F convection).
2 Place fish in large ovenproof dish. Sprinkle herbs into each fish cavity. Coat fish with oil-spray; cover with lemon slices.
3 Place tomato and ½ cup water around fish in dish; roast, uncovered, about 25 minutes or until fish is cooked through.

We used basil, parsley and oregano; use any combination of herbs you like.

salmon in cashew butter

½ cup cashews

6 tablespoons butter

⅓ cup finely chopped fresh cilantro

4 salmon fillets (6 ounces each)

prep + cook time 35 minutes
serves 4

1 Toast nuts in large dry skillet over medium-high heat, shaking pan constantly, until fragrant; remove from heat. When cool enough to handle, chop nuts coarsely.
2 Melt butter in same pan; cook nuts and cilantro, stirring, for 1 minute. Add fish to pan; cook, turning halfway through cooking, until cooked through.
3 Serve fish drizzled with butter.

barbecued salmon

3 lemons

2¾-pound side of salmon, skin off, bones removed

2 tablespoons finely chopped fresh flat-leaf parsley

1 cup dry white wine

prep + cook time 45 minutes
serves 10

1 Prepare outdoor grill for indirect cooking.
2 Thinly slice 2 of the lemons; finely grate zest from remaining lemon (you need 2 teaspoons of zest).
3 Place lemon slices in 13½-inch x 18-inch deep disposable aluminium foil pan; top with salmon. Combine zest, parsley and wine; pour over salmon, cover with foil. Place pan on covered grill, using indirect heat, following manufacturer's instructions, for about 20 minutes or until cooked to your liking. Remove salmon from grill, cover with foil; stand 10 minutes before serving.

Serve with tzatziki, if desired. For even cooking, fold the tail of the fish under so that both ends of the salmon are roughly the same thickness. For indoor cooking, bake at 350°F (325°F convection) for about the same time.

salmon with wasabi mayonnaise

4 salmon fillets (8 ounces
 each), skin on
½ cup mayonnaise
2 teaspoons wasabi paste
1 teaspoon finely chopped
 fresh cilantro

prep + cook time 20 minutes
serves 4

1 Cook fish, skin-side down, in heated oiled
 large skillet until skin crisps. Turn fish;
 cook, uncovered, until cooked through.
2 Meanwhile, combine mayonnaise, wasabi
 and cilantro in small bowl.
3 Serve fish with wasabi mayonnaise and,
 if desired, watercress and lime wedges.

salmon with creamy dill sauce

4 salmon fillets (8 ounces
 each), skin on
1 small onion, finely chopped
1 cup heavy cream
1 tablespoon coarsely chopped
 fresh dill

prep + cook time 25 minutes
serves 4

1 Cook fish, skin-side down, in heated oiled grill
 pan about 5 minutes. Turn fish; cook about
 3 minutes. Remove fish from pan; cover to
 keep warm.
2 Meanwhile, combine onion and cream in small
 saucepan; simmer, uncovered, 8 minutes then
 stir in dill.
3 Serve fish drizzled with sauce.

salmon with wasabi mayonnaise

tip Salmon is an important food to include in your weekly diet because it is low in saturated fat and high in protein. It's also a rich source of omega-3 essential fatty acids plus niacin and vitamin B12.

salmon with creamy dill sauce

tip Salmon has a wonderfully moist, delicate flavor that is beautifully complemented by this dill sauce. Make sure you get the skin nice and crispy before flipping the fillet.

baked potatoes with salmon and peas

4 large russet potatoes (about 2½ pounds), unpeeled
½ cup frozen peas
½ cup sour cream
¼ pound smoked salmon, chopped coarsely

prep + cook time 1 hour 20 minutes
serves 4

1 Preheat oven to 375°F (350°F convection).
2 Pierce potato skins with fork; wrap each potato in foil, place on oven tray. Bake about 1 hour or until tender.
3 Meanwhile, boil, steam or microwave peas until tender; drain.
4 Remove potatoes from oven; fold back foil to reveal tops of potatoes. Increase temperature to 475°F (450°F convection).
5 Cut ½ inch from top of each potato; discard. Carefully scoop out flesh from potatoes, leaving skins intact. Combine potato flesh with sour cream in medium bowl; mash potato mixture until almost smooth. Stir in peas and salmon.
6 Divide potato mixture among potato shells. Bake about 10 minutes or until browned lightly.

tuna and tomato pasta

¾ pound angel hair pasta
1 can (12 ounces) tuna packed in oil
4 cloves garlic, thinly sliced
1 can (15 ounces) canned chopped tomatoes

prep + cook time 15 minutes
serves 4

1 Cook pasta in large pot of boiling water until tender; drain, reserving ¼ cup cooking liquid. Rinse pasta under cold water, drain.
2 Meanwhile, drain tuna, reserving 2 tablespoons of the oil. Heat oil in medium skillet, add garlic; cook, stirring, until fragrant.
3 Add undrained tomatoes, tuna and reserved cooking liquid to skillet; simmer until liquid has reduced slightly. Combine pasta and sauce in large bowl.

Serve pasta with lemon wedges and basil leaves, if desired.

baked potatoes with salmon and peas

tip This is a great little meal combining all the four food groups in one stomach-satisfying package. You can use refrigerated smoked salmon or canned smoked salmon fillets, located with the canned fish in the supermarket.

tuna and tomato pasta

tips Baby capers and chopped basil can be added to the pasta sauce. Use spaghetti rather than the angel hair pasta, if that's what you've got in the cupboard.

moroccan baked spiced fish

4 whole white fish
(12 ounces each)
⅓ cup Moroccan seasoning
8 tablespoons (1 stick) butter,
softened
¼ cup coarsely chopped fresh
herbs

prep + cook time 40 minutes
serves 4

1 Preheat oven to 425°F (400°F convection).
2 Score fish through the thickest part on both
sides; sprinkle with seasoning. Cook fish, in
batches, on stove top, in heated oiled large
skillet until skin is crisp. Place fish on baking
sheet lined with parchment paper. Bake,
uncovered, about 20 minutes or until cooked
through.
3 Meanwhile, combine butter and herbs in small
bowl; season to taste.
4 Serve fish with herb butter.

*Serve with mixed salad leaves and lemon wedges,
if desired.*

lemon and fennel snapper

2 lemons
3 baby fennel bulbs
4 whole baby snapper
(12 ounces each)

prep + cook time 40 minutes
serves 4

1 Preheat oven to 425°F (400°F convection).
2 Thinly slice 1 lemon; finely grate zest from
remaining lemon (you need 2 teaspoons of
zest), then juice lemon (you need ¼ cup juice).
3 Quarter fennel lengthways; chop and reserve
1 tablespoon fennel tips.
4 Lightly coat large shallow baking dish with oil;
add fennel. Roast fennel, uncovered, 20 minutes.
5 Meanwhile, score fish three times each side.
Rub fish all over with zest; fill fish cavity with
lemon slices. Roast fish on top of fennel about
20 minutes or until fish is cooked through.
6 Serve fish and fennel sprinkled with juice and
reserved fennel tips.

moroccan baked spiced fish

tips We used snapper in this recipe, but any whole plate-sized white fish will be fine. Use any herbs you like. We used a mixture of tarragon, chervil, lemon thyme, dill and chives.

lemon and fennel snapper

tip Add a few sliced potatoes when roasting the fennel. If they are not sliced too thickly they should take about the same amount of time.

snapper with spicy butter

8 tablespoons (1 stick) butter, softened

2 tablespoons coarsely chopped drained sun-dried tomatoes in oil

1 teaspoon red pepper flakes

8 snapper fillets (6 ounces each), skin on

prep + cook time 20 minutes (+ refrigeration)
serves 8

1 Combine butter, tomato and red pepper flakes in small bowl. Place mixture on piece of plastic wrap, shape into rectangular block, wrap tightly; place in refrigerator until firm.

2 Meanwhile, cook fillets, skin side down, in heated oiled large skillet until skin is crisp; turn and cook until done as desired. Serve fish with butter.

crunchy wasabi-crusted fish

4 white fish fillets (6 ounces each)

2 tablespoons mayonnaise

2 teaspoons wasabi

½ cup panko breadcrumbs

prep + cook time 20 minutes
serves 8

1 Preheat oven to 425°F (400°F convection). Line baking sheet with parchment paper.

2 Place fish on sheet; spread with combined mayonnaise and wasabi. Press breadcrumbs onto fish. Lightly spray with oil. Roast, uncovered, about 15 minutes or until cooked through.

garlic and paprika grilled shrimp

1 pound uncooked large shrimp
⅓ cup olive oil
2 cloves garlic, crushed
1 teaspoon smoked paprika

prep + cook time 30 minutes
serves 4

1 Shell and devein shrimp, leaving tails intact.
2 Combine shrimp, oil, garlic and paprika in medium bowl.
3 Cook shrimp on heated oiled grill pan over medium-high heat until just changed in color.

shrimp and chorizo skewers

24 uncooked large shrimp
8 stalks (8 inches long) fresh rosemary
4 cloves garlic, thinly sliced
2 chorizo sausages (5 ounces each), thickly sliced

prep + cook time 25 minutes
serves 4

1 Shell and devein shrimp, leaving tails intact.
2 Remove leaves from bottom two-thirds of each rosemary stalk; thread shrimp, garlic and chorizo, alternately, onto rosemary skewers.
3 Cook skewers in heated oiled grill pan until shrimp change colur and chorizo is browned.

garlic shrimp

2 pounds uncooked large
  shrimp
4 cloves garlic, crushed
½ cup dry white wine
1 cup heavy cream

prep + cook time 15 minutes
serves 6

1 Shell and devein shrimp, leaving tails intact.
2 Heat oiled large skillet; cook shrimp and garlic, stirring, until shrimp change color. Add wine, simmer, uncovered, until liquid is reduced by half.
3 Add cream to pan; simmer, uncovered, until mixture is slightly thickened. Season to taste.

shrimp and haloumi kebabs

24 uncooked shrimp (about
   1 pound), shelled, deveined
4 ounces haloumi cheese, cut
  into 16 chunks
1 tablespoon dried oregano
8 fresh bay leaves, halved

prep + cook time 20 minutes
serves 4

1 Combine shrimp, cheese and oregano in shallow bowl; gently toss to coat. Thread shrimp, leaves and cheese alternately onto 8 small skewers; season with pepper.
2 Heat an oiled pan over medium-high; cook skewers until shrimp change color.
3 Serve immediately.

Serve with lemon wedges and bread, if desired

garlic shrimp

shrimp and haloumi kebabs

tip If you have time, combine the shrimp and garlic in a bowl and refrigerate, covered, up to 2 hours ahead to marinate for extra flavor.

tips You'll need 8 small wooden skewers for this recipe. Soak the skewers in water for 30 minutes before using to prevent them scorching and splintering.

shrimp stir-fry

2 pounds uncooked large
  shrimp
1 large red bell pepper,
  thickly sliced
1 cup prepared satay sauce
3 scallions, thinly sliced

prep + cook time 20 minutes
serves 4

1 Shell and devein shrimp, leaving tails intact.
2 Heat oiled wok; stir-fry shrimp and bell
  peppers until shrimp change color. Add sauce
  and scallions; stir-fry until hot.

steamed mussels in
tomato garlic broth

4 cloves garlic, crushed
1 can (15 ounces) diced
  tomatoes
4 pounds small black mussels
½ cup coarsely chopped fresh
  flat-leaf parsley

prep + cook time 30 minutes
serves 4

1 Cook garlic in oiled large saucepan, stirring, until
  soft. Add undrained tomatoes and ½ cup water;
  bring to a boil. Reduce heat; simmer, uncovered,
  about 5 minutes or until sauce thickens slightly.
2 Meanwhile, scrub mussels; remove beards. Add
  mussels to pan; simmer, covered, about 5 minutes,
  shaking pan occasionally, until mussels open
  (discard any that do not). Remove mussels from
  pan, divide among serving bowls; cover with foil
  to keep warm.
3 Bring tomato mixture to a boil; boil, uncovered,
  about 5 minutes or until slightly thickened. Pour
  tomato mixture over mussels; sprinkle with parsley.

tip You can use any firm white fish in this recipe. Snapper and cod are both good choices. Remove any small bones with tweezers.

shrimp stir-fry

tip Mussels should be alive until they reach the pot, as they quickly become toxic after they die. Fresh, live mussels will be closed or should close quickly when tapped. If they remain open, discard them.

steamed mussels in tomato garlic broth

mussels in thai broth

2 pounds medium black mussels

¼ cup red Thai curry paste

1 can (15 ounces) coconut milk

1 cup firmly packed fresh cilantro leaves

prep + cook time 35 minutes
serves 4

1 Scrub mussels; remove beards.
2 Cook curry paste in heated oiled wok, stirring, until fragrant. Add coconut milk and 2½ cups water; bring to a boil. Reduce heat; simmer, covered, 10 minutes or until broth thickens slightly.
3 Add mussels; simmer, covered, about 5 minutes or until mussels open (discard any that do not).
4 Serve bowls of soup sprinkled with cilantro.

broiled mussels with prosciutto

1 pound small black mussels

8 tablespoons (1 stick) butter, softened

¼ pound thinly sliced prosciutto, finely chopped

4 scallions, finely chopped

prep + cook time 30 minutes
serves 4

1 Scrub mussels; remove beards. Bring 2 cups water to a boil in large saucepan. Add the mussels, cover; boil about 3 minutes or until mussels open (discard any that do not).
2 Drain mussels; discard liquid. Break open shells; discard top shell. Loosen mussels from shells with a spoon; return mussels to shells, place, in single layer, on baking sheet.
3 Preheat broiler.
4 Combine butter, prosciutto and onion in small bowl. Divide butter mixture over mussels; broil about 3 minutes or until lightly browned.

chili salt and pepper seafood stir-fry

2 pounds mixed seafood
2 teaspoons sea salt
½ teaspoon five-spice powder
2 fresh small red Thai chilies, finely chopped

prep + cook time 25 minutes
serves 4

1 Shell and devein shrimps, leaving tails intact.
2 Combine seafood, salt, five-spice and chiles in large bowl.
3 Stir-fry seafood in oiled wok over high heat, in batches, until cooked. Serve immediately.

We used uncooked shrimps, calamari and scallops; you can use any combination of seafood you like.

peri-peri calamari

1½ pound frozen calamari, thawed
2 tablespoons peri-peri spice mix
½ cup cornmeal
⅔ cup mayonnaise

prep + cook time 30 minutes
serves 4

1 Reserve 1 teaspoon spice mix. Pat dry calamari and combine with remaining spice mix in large bowl.
2 Toss calamari in cornmeal; deep-fry calamari in wok of hot oil, in batches, until lightly browned and tender. Drain.
3 Meanwhile, combine mayonnaise and reserved spice mix in small bowl; accompany with calamari.

crab spaghetti in a bag

3/4 pound spaghetti

2 cups prepared marinara sauce

1 can (8 ounces) cooked crab meat

2 tablespoons finely chopped fresh flat-leaf parsley

prep + cook time 35 minutes
serves 6

1 Cook pasta in large pot of boiling water, until almost tender; drain.
2 Preheat oven to 375°F (350°F convection).
3 Combine sauce, crab, parsley and ½ cup water in large bowl. Add pasta; mix well.
4 Place a double layer of parchment paper (or foil), cut into 10-inch squares, into small bowl; fill with one fourth of the pasta mixture. Gather corners of paper together above pasta mixture to enclose completely; secure with kitchen string to form a bag. Repeat to make a total of 4 bags.
5 Place bags on baking sheet; bake 15 minutes. Remove string before serving; open carefully so stem is directed away from you.

lemon tarragon scallop skewers

2 lemons

24 scallops (about 1¼ pounds)

2 teaspoons olive oil

2 teaspoons finely chopped fresh tarragon

prep + cook time 15 minutes
serves 4

1 Cut one lemon into eight wedges. Juice remaining lemon (you need 2 tablespoons).
2 Thread one lemon wedge onto each of eight bamboo skewers. Thread scallops onto skewers.
3 Spray heated barbecue grill plate with oil-spray. Cook skewers over medium-high heat about 1 minute each side or until cooked through.
4 Combine juice, oil and tarragon in small bowl; serve scallops drizzled with dressing.

Soak the skewers in cold water for 30 minutes before using to prevent them from splintering and scorching during cooking.

crab spaghetti in a bag

tip Crab meat is available in the seafood section of most supermarkets.

lemon tarragon scallop skewers

tip Tarragon is known as the 'king of herbs' by the French, as it is the essential flavoring for many of their classic sauces. It has a mild aniseed flavor and goes particularly well with many French dishes, but especially egg, seafood and chicken recipes.

Salsas

These salsas are great served with grilled fish and seafood, as well as poultry and beef.

pear, pistachio, parsley and orange salsa

2 pears, finely chopped

¼ cup shelled pistachios, toasted, finely chopped

¼ cup finely chopped fresh flat-leaf parsley

2 tablespoons orange juice

1 Combine ingredients in small bowl.

prep time 10 minutes
serves 4

fennel, yellow tomato, roasted pepper and lemon salsa

1 large fennel bulb

½ cup roasted red bell pepper in oil

yellow grape tomatoes, quartered

2 tablespoons lemon juice

1 Remove fronds from fennel; chop finely (you need 2 tablespoons). Chop fennel finely.

2 Drain bell pepper reserving 1 tablespoon of the oil. Chop bell pepper finely.

3 Combine fennel, fronds, bell pepper, tomatoes, juice and reserved oil in small bowl.

prep time 10 minutes
serves 4

Fennel fronds are the delicate feathery tips of the fennel plant. They have a light flavor.

pineapple, cucumber, lime and chile salsa

½ small pineapple, finely chopped

1 small cucumber, seeded and finely chopped

1 fresh long red chile, finely chopped

2 tablespoons lime juice

1 Combine ingredients in small bowl.

prep time 10 minutes

serves 4

peanut, chili, cilantro and lime salsa

½ cup coarsely chopped roasted peanuts

2 tablespoons finely chopped fresh cilantro

1 tablespoon sweet chilli sauce

1 tablespoon lime juice

1 Combine ingredients in small bowl.

prep time 10 minutes

serves 4

Poultry

Here's your chance to really shine. Whether you're planning a casual summer barbecue or need a quick weeknight meal to share with friends, these speedy main dishes will help you pull together a memorable dinner with ease.

34

chicken with roasted cherry tomato and basil sauce

1 pound cherry tomatoes

4 boneless, skinless chicken breasts (6 ounces each)

¼ cup coarsely chopped fresh basil

¼ cup heavy cream

prep + cook time 35 minutes
serves 4

1 Preheat oven to 400°F (375°F convection).

2 Place tomatoes in large shallow baking dish; spray with cooking-oil spray. Roast, uncovered, about 20 minutes or until tomatoes soften.

3 Meanwhile, cook chicken in heated oiled large skillet until cooked through. Cover; stand 5 minutes.

4 Blend or process half the tomatoes until smooth. Place in medium saucepan with basil and cream; cook, stirring, over low heat, until heated through. Serve chicken topped with sauce and remaining tomatoes.

pesto chicken with grilled zucchini

6 medium zucchini, thickly sliced lengthways

1 teaspoon fresh lemon zest

⅓ cup sun-dried tomato pesto

4 boneless skinless chicken thighs (6 ounces each), cut into thirds

prep + cook time 25 minutes
serves 4

1 Coat zucchini with cooking oil-spray; cook in heated oiled grill pan, in batches, until tender. Place zucchini in medium bowl; sprinkle with zest. Cover to keep warm.

2 Combine pesto and chicken in large bowl. Cook chicken on heated oiled grill pan, until cooked through. Serve chicken with zucchini.

Serve with baby arugula or a leafy green salad, if desired.

chicken with cherry tomato and basil sauce

tip Basil is one of the easiest and most useful herbs to grow. You don't need a large kitchen garden: a pot or a window box in a protected, sunny position is sufficient. Basil will grow year-round (depending on the climate) and you can freeze the leaves for later use.

pesto chicken with grilled zucchini

tip Salmon has a wonderfully moist, delicate flavor that is beautifully complemented by this dill sauce. Make sure you get the skin nice and crispy before flipping the fillet.

herb-crumbed chicken breasts

4 boneless skinless chicken
breasts (6 ounces each))
1½ cups fresh breadcrumbs
3 tablespoons butter, melted
¼ cup finely chopped fresh
mixed herbs

prep + cook time 30 minutes
serves 4

1 Cook chicken in heated oiled large skillet until
cooked through; place on oven tray.
2 Meanwhile, combine breadcrumbs, butter and
herbs in small bowl.
3 Preheat broiler. Sprinkle breadcrumb mixture
over chicken; brown lightly under broiler.

*Use fresh herbs such as basil, chives, parsley
and rosemary.*

chicken with capers and lemon

4 chicken breast cutlets
(4 ounces each)
2 tablespoons lemon juice
⅓ cup chicken stock
2 tablespoons rinsed, drained,
capers, coarsely chopped

prep + cook time 20 minutes
serves 4

1 Cook chicken in heated oiled large skillet until
browned both sides and cooked through.
Remove from pan; cover to keep warm.
2 Add juice and stock to skillet; bring to a boil.
Reduce heat; simmer, uncovered, 1 minute. Stir
in capers. Slice chicken and serve with sauce.

chicken saltimbocca

4 chicken breast cutlets
(about 4 ounces each)
4 fresh sage leaves
4 slices prosciutto
1 cup dry white wine

prep + cook time 20 minutes
serves 4

1 Roll each chicken cutlet, top with sage leaves. Wrap one prosciutto slice around each roll; secure with toothpicks or small skewers.
2 Cook chicken in heated oiled large skillet, prosciutto seam-side down, turning occasionally, until cooked. Remove from pan.
3 Pour wine into skillet; bring to a boil, stirring. Boil until liquid is reduced by half. Drizzle chicken saltimbocca with sauce.

gorgonzola and sage-stuffed chicken

⅓ cup semi-dried tomatoes
in oil
4 boneless, skinless chicken
breasts
3 ounces gorgonzola cheese,
cut into four even slices
12 fresh sage leaves

prep + cook time 25 minutes
serves 4

1 Drain tomatoes; reserve 2 tablespoons of the oil.
2 Cut horizontal slits into chicken fillets, three-quarters of the way through, to make pockets. Divide cheese, sage and tomatoes among pockets.
3 Cook chicken in heated oiled large skillet until cooked through. Slice chicken thickly.

chicken yakitori

1 pound chicken tenderloins
½ cup mirin
¼ cup soy sauce
1 teaspoon toasted sesame
   seeds

prep + cook time
30 minutes (plus refrigeration time)
makes 24

You need 16 bamboo skewers for this recipe. Soak in water for at least an hour before using to avoid scorching and splintering during cooking.

1 Thread tenderloins loosely onto skewers. Place skewers, in single layer, in large shallow dish.
2 Combine mirin and soy in small bowl. Pour half the marinade over skewers; reserve remaining marinade. Cover; refrigerate 3 hours or overnight.
3 Simmer reserved marinade in small saucepan over low heat until reduced by half.
4 Meanwhile, cook drained skewers in heated oiled grill pan until chicken is cooked through.
5 Serve skewers drizzled with hot marinade and sprinkled with sesame seeds.

thai chicken burgers

2 cups baby asian greens
1 pound ground chicken
¼ cup Thai chili sauce
4 ciabatta bread rolls,
   split, toasted

prep + cook time 20 minutes
serves 4

1 Chop half the asian greens finely; place in medium bowl with chicken and 1 tablespoon of the chili sauce. Mix well; shape into four patties.
2 Cook patties in heated oiled large skillet until cooked through.
3 Sandwich patties, remaining greens and chili sauce between bun halves.

chicken yakitori

tip Mirin is a sweet rice wine used in Japanese cooking. There are two types of Mirin—Hon Mirin with an alcohol level of 14% and Shin Mirin containing less than 1% alcohol—and they are widely available in supermarkets and Asian grocery stores. We use Shin Mirin in our recipes, unless otherwise stated.

thai chicken burgers

tip Thai chili sauce, a sweet and spicy Asian condiment, is typically available in the international food section of most grocery stores.

portuguese lime chicken thigh fillets

¼ cup bottled peri-peri sauce

2 tablespoons lime juice

2 tablespoons finely chopped fresh cilantro

8 boneless, skinless chicken thighs (4 ounces each)

prep + cook time 20 minutes
serves 4

1 Combine sauce, juice and cilantro in large bowl. Add chicken; toss to coat in mixture.
2 Cook chicken in heated oiled grill pan until browned and cooked through.

spiced grilled chicken

¼ cup lemon juice

1 teaspoon ground cumin

2 teaspoons sweet paprika

8 boneless, skinless chicken thighs (4 ounces each)

prep + cook time 30 minutes
serves 4

1 Combine juice, spices and chicken in medium bowl.
2 Cook chicken in heated oiled grill pan until cooked through.

Serve with tomato chutney, if desired. Chicken thighs are fattier than breasts, but this does makes them juicier.

balsamic chicken

¼ cup balsamic vinegar

2 tablespoons olive oil

1 tablespoon fresh rosemary leaves

8 boneless, skinless chicken thighs (4 ounces each)

prep + cook time 15 minutes
serves 4

1 Combine vinegar, oil and rosemary in medium bowl, add chicken; toss to coat in marinade.

2 Drain chicken; reserve marinade. Cook chicken in heated oiled grill pan until cooked through.

roast lemon and cumin chicken

2 lemons

2 tablespoons olive oil

1 tablespoon ground cumin

1 whole chicken (about 4 pounds)

prep + cook time 1 hour 35 minutes (plus standing time)
serves 4

1 Preheat oven to 400°F (375°F convection).

2 Juice one lemon (you need 2 tablespoons); cut remaining lemon into wedges.

3 Combine oil, cumin and juice in small bowl. Place lemon wedges in cavity of chicken. Rub skin all over with cumin mixture; tie chicken legs together with kitchen string.

4 Half fill large baking dish with water; place chicken on oiled wire rack over dish. Roast 20 minutes. Reduce oven temperature to 350°F (325°F convection); roast chicken about 1 hour or until cooked through. Remove chicken from rack; cover, stand 20 minutes before serving.

pan-fried chicken with spicy butter

- 4 tablespoons butter, softened
- ½ teaspoon dried red pepper flakes
- 1 tablespoon coarsely chopped drained sun-dried tomatoes in oil
- 4 boneless, skinless chicken thighs (about 6 ounces each)

1 Combine butter, pepper flakes and tomatoes in small bowl. Place mixture on piece of plastic wrap, shape into rectangular block, wrap tightly; place in refrigerator until firm.

2 Meanwhile, cook chicken in heated oiled large skillet until browned both sides and cooked through. Serve chicken with butter slices, and roasted potato wedges, if desired.

prep + cook time
25 minutes (plus refrigeration time)
serves 4

mexican-style chicken

- 4 chicken breast fillets (about 6 ounces each)
- 1 packet (10 ounce) taco seasoning mix
- 1 fresh small red Thai chile, finely chopped
- 1 tablespoon lime juice

1 Combine ingredients in medium bowl; refrigerate 10 minutes.

2 Cook chicken in heated oiled large skillet until browned both sides and cooked through. Serve with grilled corn, if desired.

prep + cook time 25 minutes
serves 4

thai red curry chicken

2 tablespoons Thai red curry
  paste
1/3 cup loosely packed fresh
  cilantro leaves
1/2 cup coconut milk
4 boneless, skinless chicken
  breasts (about 6 ounces each

prep + cook time 20 minutes
serves 4

1 Blend or process curry paste, cilantro and
  coconut milk until smooth. Combine curry
  mixture and chicken in medium bowl; toss
  to coat chicken in mixture.
2 Cook chicken in heated oiled grill pan until
  browned both sides. Cover; cook 10 minutes
  or until cooked through.
3 If you like, sprinkle the chicken with cilantro
  and serve with steamed jasmine rice.

sesame wasabi chicken

1 tablespoon soy sauce
1 tablespoon sesame oil
2 tablespoons wasabi paste
8 chicken drumsticks
  (about 2 1/2 pounds)

prep + cook time 50 minutes
serves 4

1 Combine sauce, oil and wasabi in large bowl,
  add chicken; turn to coat in mixture.
2 Cook chicken in heated oiled grill pan, about
  40 minutes or until cooked through.

sumac and sesame chicken skewers

1¼ pounds boneless, skinless
    chicken breast, cut into
    1-inch cubes
1 tablespoon sumac
1 teaspoon sesame seeds
1 teaspoon black sesame seeds

prep + cook time 30 minutes
serves 4

1 Thread chicken onto 16 small bamboo
   skewers.
2 Combine sumac and seeds in small bowl;
   sprinkle sumac mixture all over skewers.
3 Cook skewers in heated oiled grill pan until
   chicken is cooked through.

*Soak the skewers in cold water for 30 minutes
before using to prevent them from splintering
and scorching during cooking.*

chicken and mushrooms in oyster sauce

1¼ pounds boneless, skinless
    chicken breast, thinly sliced
1 pound mixed mushrooms,
    coarsely chopped
½ pound baby bok choy,
    coarsely chopped
⅓ cup oyster sauce

prep + cook time 20 minutes
serves 4

1 Heat oiled wok; stir-fry chicken, in batches,
   until cooked through; remove from wok.
2 Add mushrooms; stir-fry until tender. Add
   bok choy, sauce and 2 tablespoons water;
   stir-fry until vegetables are tender.

tip Sumac is a purple-red spice ground from berries growing on shrubs that flourish wild around the Mediterranean; it has a mild, tart, lemony flavor. Try serving these skewers with lemon wedges for an extra zing.

sumac and sesame chicken skewers

tip We used fresh shiitake, oyster and enoki mushrooms in this recipe, but you can use any combination you like.

chicken and mushrooms in oyster sauce

34

Meats

At the end of the day when time is limited, energy is depleted and everyone is hungry, these hearty meat dishes mean that dinner can be on the table with minimum fuss.

beef sirloin with herb butter

4 tablespoons butter, softened

1 clove garlic

¼ cup finely chopped fresh mixed herbs

4 beef sirloin steaks (8 ounces each)

prep + cook time 30 minutes (plus refrigeration time)

serves 4

1 Place butter, garlic and herbs in small bowl; stir until combined. Place on piece of plastic wrap, shape into a rectangular block; wrap tightly, refrigerate until firm.

2 Cook beef in heated oiled large skillet until browned both sides and cooked as desired. Cover; stand 5 minutes. Top steaks with butter. Serve with oven-roasted fries, if desired.

grilled steaks with anchovy butter

4 New-York cut steaks (7 ounces each)

6 tablespoons butter, softened

4 drained anchovy fillets, coarsely chopped

2 tablespoons finely chopped fresh flat-leaf parsley

prep + cook time 20 minutes

serves 6

1 Cook steaks in heated grill pan until cooked as desired. Cover steaks; stand 5 minutes.

2 Meanwhile, combine butter, anchovy and parsley in small bowl.

3 Serve steaks topped with anchovy butter.

Serve with oven-roasted potato wedges and a tossed green salad.

beef sirloin with herb butter

grilled steaks with anchovy butter

tip Use herbs such as parsley, basil and chives. Sirloin is a full-flavored steak and is considered one of the cheaper of the premium steaks. Instead of the sirloin you could use rib eye, porterhouse or tenderloin.

tip New-York cut steak is sometimes sold as boneless sirloin. You can make the anchovy butter well ahead of time and keep it in the freezer.

chili-rubbed hickory-smoked rib-eye steaks

You need 1 cup hickory chips and a smoke box, available at most stores where grills are sold.

- 1 tablespoon fresh lemon zest
- 2 teaspoons chili powder
- 2 tablespoons olive oil
- 4 beef rib-eye steaks (8 ounces each)

prep + cook time 20 minutes (plus refrigeration and standing time)
serves 4

1 Combine zest, chili powder and oil in large bowl with steaks. Cover; refrigerate 3 hours or overnight.
2 Cover hickory chips with 2 cups water in medium bowl; stand 3 hours or overnight.
3 Place drained smoking chips in smoke box alongside steaks in covered outdoor grill. Follow manufacturer's instructions, using indirect heat to cook steaks, about 10 minutes or as desired.

barbecue and honey steak

- 2 tablespoons barbecue sauce
- 1 tablespoon Worcestershire sauce
- 1 tablespoon honey
- 4 New-York cut sirloin steaks

prep + cook time 25 minutes
serves 4

1 Combine sauces and honey in large bowl, add beef; turn to coat in mixture.
2 Cook beef in heated oiled grill pan until browned both sides and cooked as desired.

bacon-wrapped steaks with tarragon butter

- 4 tablespoons butter, softened
- 2 teaspoons finely chopped fresh tarragon
- ½ pound bacon
- 4 beef tenderloin steaks (6 ounces each)

prep + cook time 30 minutes (plus refrigeration time)
serves 4

1 Combine butter and tarragon in small bowl. Place on piece of plastic wrap; shape into 2½-inch log, wrap tightly. Refrigerate until firm.
2 Wrap bacon around steaks; secure with toothpicks. Cook steaks, uncovered, in heated oiled large skillet, until cooked as desired. Cover steaks; stand 5 minutes.
3 Serve steaks topped with butter.

steak with mustard cream

- 2 pound piece beef tenderloin, cut into four steaks
- ¾ cup dry white wine
- 8 ounces crème fraîche
- 1 tablespoon wholegrain mustard

prep + cook time 30 minutes
serves 4

1 Heat oiled large skillet; cook steaks, in batches, until browned both sides and cooked as desired. Transfer to a plate and cover to keep warm.
2 Place wine in same skillet; bring to boil, stirring. Reduce heat; simmer, uncovered, 1 minute. Whisk in crème fraîche and mustard; simmer, uncovered, about 2 minutes or until sauce thickens slightly.
3 Drizzle steaks with the sauce; serve with roasted potatoes, if desired.

grilled steak with baba ghanoush

4 beef tenderloin steaks
  (6 ounces each)
2 red bell peppers, thickly
  sliced
2 large zucchini, sliced thinly
  lengthways
½ cup baba ghanoush

prep + cook time 35 minutes
serves 4

1 Coat steaks and vegetables with cooking-oil spray. Cook steaks and vegetables in heated grill pan in batches, until steaks are cooked as desired and vegetables are tender.
2 Divide vegetables among serving plates, top with steaks. Serve with baba ghanoush, and fresh mint, if desired.

peppered beef steaks

4 beef tenderloin steaks
  (6 ounces each)
2 tablespoons drained green
  peppercorns
½ cup heavy cream
⅔ cup beef stock

prep + cook time 25 minutes
serves 4

1 Cook beef in heated oiled large skillet until cooked as desired. Remove from heat; cover to keep warm.
2 Add peppercorns, cream and stock to skillet; bring to a boil. Reduce heat; simmer, uncovered, until slightly thickened.

grilled steak with baba ghanoush

tip Considered a cut above the rest, tenderloin (also known as filet mignon) steaks are the most tender cut of beef. They are best cooked hot and fast.

peppered beef steaks

tip Serve these juicy peppery steaks with roasted baby carrots and steamed or microwaved crunchy broccolini.

beef with red wine

4 cloves garlic

3 cups dry red wine

8 sprigs fresh thyme

1¼-pound piece tenderloin beef, trimmed, tied at 1-inch intervals

prep + cook time 30 minutes
serves 4

1 Bruise unpeeled garlic by hitting with the flat blade of a heavy knife.
2 Combine garlic, wine, 2 cups of water and thyme in large deep saucepan; bring to a boil, boil 5 minutes. Add beef; simmer, uncovered, about 30 minutes or until cooked as desired, turning beef once. Remove beef, wrap in foil; stand 10 minutes.
3 Serve beef thickly sliced.

The beef will be medium-rare if cooked for 20 minutes.

peppered steak

1¼-pound piece tenderloin beef, trimmed

2 teaspoons Dijon mustard

2 teaspoons cracked black pepper

prep + cook time 35 minutes
serves 4

1 Preheat oven to 425°F (400°F convection).
2 Coat beef in mustard and pepper. Heat large oiled skillet; brown beef all over.
3 Place beef into heated oiled baking dish; transfer to oven. Roast beef, uncovered, about 20 minutes or until cooked as desired. Cover loosely with foil; stand 10 minutes, before slicing.

herb beef skewers

1⅓ pounds beef sirloin, thickly
   sliced
2 tablespoons finely chopped
   fresh flat-leaf parsley
2 tablespoons wholegrain
   mustard

prep + cook time 25 minutes
(+ refrigeration) **serves** 4

1 Thread equal amounts of beef onto each of
  8 skewers. Using fingers, press combined
  parsley and mustard all over beef, cover
  skewers; refrigerate 30 minutes.
2 Cook beef skewers in heated oiled large skillet
  until lightly browned and cooked though.

*Soak bamboo skewers in cold water for at least
30 minutes before using to prevent them from
splintering and scorching during cooking.*

spicy beef noodles

½ pound dried rice noodles
1¼ pounds beef sirloin, thinly
   sliced
2 tablespoons thai chili sauce
1½ pounds packaged fresh
   stir-fry vegetables

prep + cook time 25 minutes
serves 4

1 Place noodles in large heatproof
  bowl, cover with boiling water;
  stand until tender, drain.

2 Meanwhile, combine beef and half the chili
  sauce in medium bowl.
3 Stir-fry beef, in batches, in heated oiled wok
  until browned; remove from wok.
4 Add vegetables to wok; stir-fry until tender.
  Return beef to wok with noodles, ¼ cup water
  and remaining chili sauce; stir-fry until hot.
  Season to taste.

*Serve sprinkled with thai basil, if desired.
Thai chili sauce is a combination of garlic,
shallots, chilli, tomato paste, fish sauce, galangal,
spices and shrimp paste. It is sold under various
names, and can be found in Asian food stores.*

veal schnitzels
with mustard cream

8 thin veal cutlets
  (3 ounces each)
½ cup dry white wine
½ cup cream
2 teaspoons wholegrain
  mustard

prep + cook time 20 minutes
serves 4

1 Cook veal in heated oiled large skillet,
  in batches, until cooked as desired. Cover to
  keep warm.
2 Add wine to same pan; cook, stirring, until
  reduced by half. Add cream and mustard;
  simmer, uncovered, about 3 minutes or until
  sauce thickens slightly. Serve veal with sauce.

*Serve with fried potatoes and bacon, or
a leafy green salad.*

veal saltimbocca

4 veal cutlets (4 ounces each)
4 fresh sage leaves
4 thick slices center cut bacon
1 cup dry white wine

prep + cook time 20 minutes
serves 4

1 Roll each cutlet, top with sage leaves. Wrap
  one bacon strip around each roll; secure with
  toothpicks or small skewers.
2 Cook cutlets in heated oiled large skillet, bacon
  seam-side down, turning occasionally, until
  cooked. Remove from pan.
3 Pour wine into pan; bring to boil, stirring.
  Boil until liquid is reduced by half. Drizzle
  saltimbocca with sauce; serve with roasted
  potatoes, if desired.

veal schnitzels with mustard cream

tip Veal schnitzels, or escalopes, are large but very thin slices of lean veal. They are tender and quick-cooking, and are often coated with breadcrumbs and pan-fried in butter; this unbreaded version is slightly lighter, but just as delicious.

veal saltimbocca

tip Saltimbocca is a Roman specialty (the word means "jumps in the mouth"); it's made from very thin slices of meat, usually veal, topped with sage leaves and prosciutto or ham, rolled and sautéed in butter and wine.

veal chops with mustard cream

4 veal chops (6 ounces each)
¾ cup dry white wine
8 ounces crème fraîche
1 tablespoons wholegrain
  mustard

prep + cook time 30 minutes
serves 4

1 Heat oiled large skillet; cook veal until browned both sides and cooked as desired. Cover to keep warm.
2 Place wine in same skillet; bring to a boil, stirring. Reduce heat; simmer, uncovered, 2 minutes. Whisk in crème fraîche and mustard; simmer, uncovered, about 5 minutes or until sauce thickens slightly.
3 Drizzle chops with the sauce.

veal with roasted cherry tomatoes

1 pound cherry tomatoes
4 veal cutlets (4 ounces each)
¼ cup coarsely chopped fresh basil
¼ cup heavy cream

prep + cook time 35 minutes
serves 4

1 Preheat oven to 400°F (375°F convection).
2 Place tomatoes in large shallow baking dish; coat with cooking spray. Roast, uncovered, about 20 minutes or until tomatoes soften.
3 Meanwhile, cook veal in heated oiled large skillet until cooked through. Cover; stand 5 minutes.
4 Blend or process half the tomatoes until smooth. Place in medium saucepan with basil and cream; cook, stirring, over low heat, until heated through. Serve veal topped with sauce and remaining tomatoes.

veal pizzaiola

4 slices pancetta,
  finely chopped
1 jar (24 ounces) tomato pasta
  sauce
4 veal cutlets (5 ounces each)
2 cups baby spinach

prep + cook time 25 minutes
serves 4

1 Cook pancetta in oiled medium saucepan, stirring, until crisp. Add sauce; simmer, uncovered, about 15 minutes or until sauce thickens.
2 Cook veal in heated oiled grill pan until browned both sides and cooked as desired.
3 Remove sauce from heat; stir in spinach. Top veal with sauce.

Use a tomato pasta sauce with garlic and herbs for extra flavor.

veal with basil mayo

4 veal cutlets (5 ounces each)
1½ cups fresh basil
4 slices prosciutto
½ cup mayonnaise

prep + cook time 30 minutes
serves 4

1 Preheat oven to 400°F (375°F convection).
2 Oil two baking sheets. Place cutlets on one sheet; top each with 3 basil leaves and then wrap in prosciutto (securing with toothpick if necessary). Roast, uncovered, 20 minutes or until cutlets are cooked as desired.
3 Meanwhile, blend or process mayonnaise and remaining basil until smooth.
4 Serve cutlets with mayonnaise.

veal chops with grilled fennel and mandarin

4 veal chops (6 ounces each)
2 baby fennel bulbs, trimmed, halved lengthways
4 small mandarin oranges, peeled, halved horizontally
2 tablespoons prepared basil pesto

prep + cook time 25 minutes
serves 4

1 Cook veal in heated oiled grill pan until cooked.
2 Cook fennel and oranges on grill plate until just browned.
3 Top veal with pesto; serve with fennel and mandarin.

veal with lemon and oregano

2 lemons
2 cloves garlic, thinly sliced
1/4 cup fresh oregano
8 veal cutlets (3 ounces each)

prep + cook time 20 minutes
serves 4

1 Finely grate zest from one lemon (you need 1 teaspoon). Juice lemons (you need 2/3 cup).
2 Cook garlic and oregano in heated oiled large skillet, stirring, until garlic is lightly browned and oregano is crisp. Remove with a slotted spoon; drain on paper towels.
3 Cook veal in same pan, in batches, until browned both sides; remove from pan. Add zest and juice to pan; cook 1 minute.
4 Serve veal drizzled with pan juices; sprinkle with garlic and oregano mixture.

We used uncrumbed (plain) veal schnitzel in this recipe.
Serve with mixed salad leaves.

veal chops with grilled fennel and mandarin

tip Fennel is popular in French, Italian and Greek cooking and has a sweet licorice flavor. The entire fennel plant (bulb, stalks and leaves) is edible. The stalks can be used in soups and stews and the leaves (also known as fronds) can be used as a herb, providing great flavor to baked fish and poultry.

veal with lemon and oregano

tip Because veal cutlets are a very lean cut of meat, they dry out quickly if overcooked. Cook them over a high heat for as little time as possible.

lamb with pesto butter

4 tablespoons butter, softened

2 tablespoons basil pesto

12 teaspoon fresh lemon zest

4 lamb fillets (6 ounces each)

1 Stir butter, pesto and zest in small bowl until well combined.

2 Cook lamb in heated oiled large skillet until cooked as desired. Remove from skillet.

3 Serve lamb topped with a dollop of butter.

prep + cook time 20 minutes
serves 4

maple syrup-glazed lamb shanks

2 tablespoons pure maple syrup

½ cup chicken stock

¾ cup orange juice

4 French-trimmed lamb shanks (8 ounces each)

1 Combine syrup, stock and juice in large deep flameproof casserole dish, add lamb; turn lamb to coat in syrup mixture. Bring to the a then cover tightly.

2 Reduce heat, cook lamb, turning every 20 minutes, about 2 hours or until tender.

prep + cook time 2 hours 20 minutes
serves 4

greek-style barbecued lamb

5-pound leg of lamb
10 cloves garlic, halved
1/4 cup lemon juice
1/4 cup chopped fresh oregano

prep + cook time 1 hour 50 minutes
(+ standing) **serves** 10

1 Place lamb in large oiled baking dish, make slits all over with sharp knife; push garlic into slits. Season to taste. Drizzle with juice; sprinkle with oregano.

2 Cook lamb in covered outdoor grill, following manufacturer's instructions, using indirect heat, about 1 hour 40 minutes or until cooked as desired. Cover lamb; stand 20 minutes before serving.

roast lamb and potatoes

4-pound leg of lamb
3 sprigs fresh rosemary, coarsely chopped
1/2 teaspoon sweet paprika
2 pounds potatoes, coarsely chopped

prep + cook time 1 hour 20 minutes
serves 6

1 Preheat oven to 400°F (375°F convection).

2 Place lamb in oiled large baking dish; using sharp knife, score skin at 3/4-inch intervals, sprinkle with rosemary and paprika. Arrange potatoes around lamb; season to taste and spray with oil. Roast 15 minutes.

3 Reduce oven to 350°F (325°F convection); roast about 45 minutes or until lamb is cooked as desired. Remove lamb from dish; stand, loosely covered with foil, 10 minutes. Meanwhile, roast potatoes another 15 minutes or until tender.

4 Slice lamb; serve with roasted potatoes.

lamb chops with sweet citrus sauce

8 lamb chops (3 ounces each)
1 large orange
½ cup red currant jelly
1 tablespoon red wine vinegar

prep + cook time 25 minutes
serves 4

1 Cook lamb in heated oiled large skillet until cooked as desired.
2 Meanwhile, grate zest from orange (you need 1 teaspoon). Juice orange (you need ⅓ cup).
3 Combine zest, juice, jelly and vinegar in medium saucepan; stir over heat until jelly melts. Bring to a boil; reduce heat. Simmer, uncovered, until sauce thickens slightly.
4 Serve lamb with citrus sauce; accompany with mashed potatoes and arugula salad, if desired.

hoisin sweet chili lamb and vegetable stir-fry

1½ pounds lamb loin, sliced in thin strips
1 pound packaged fresh stir-fry vegetables
⅓ cup hoisin sauce
2 tablespoons sweet chili sauce

prep + cook time 15 minutes
serves 4

1 Stir-fry lamb, in batches, in heated oiled wok until cooked through.
2 Stir-fry vegetables in wok until almost tender. Return lamb to wok with sauces and 2 tablespoons water; stir-fry until hot.

lamb chops with sweet citrus sauce

tip Lamb chops are a great source of protein and the combination here of the meat with the delicately tangy flavor of the citrus sauce is a winning combination for your taste buds.

hoisin sweet chili lamb and vegetable stir-fry

tip Make sure the wok is very hot and continue to stir continuously while cooking. Don't overcook the vegetables—they should remain slightly crunchy, not soft.

pork fillet with apples

2 pounds pork tenderloins
2 apples, cut into thin wedges
2 tablespoons sugar
1 tablespoon lemon juice

prep + cook time 30 minutes
serves 8

1 Heat oiled large skillet; cook pork until browned and cooked. Remove from pan; stand, loosely covered with foil, 10 minutes.
2 Meanwhile, cook apple in same cleaned skillet, stirring, 2 minutes. Add sugar and juice; cook, stirring, about 3 minutes or until apple is browned and tender.
3 Slice pork thinly. Serve with apple; drizzle with any pan juices.

lemon pepper pork

1 lemon
4 pork cutlets (8 ounces each)
2 cups frozen fava beans
4 ounces feta cheese, crumbled

prep + cook time 35 minutes
serves 4

1 Finely grate 1 tablespoons zest from lemon. Squeeze juice from lemon (you need 2 tablespoons juice).
2 Season pork with pepper; sprinkle both sides with half the zest. Cook in heated oiled grill pan until cooked through.
3 Meanwhile, boil, steam or microwave beans until just tender; drain. When cool enough to handle, peel beans.
4 Combine beans, remaining zest, juice and cheese in large bowl. Season to taste. Serve pork with salad.

creamy garlic pork chops

4 pork chops (8 ounces each)

3 cloves garlic, crushed

1 cup heavy cream

3 tablespoons coarsely chopped fresh sage

prep + cook time 25 minutes
serves 4

1 Cook pork in heated oiled large skillet about 15 minutes or until cooked through. Remove from pan; cover to keep warm.

2 Cook garlic in same pan, stirring, 1 minute. Add cream; bring to a boil. Reduce heat; simmer, uncovered, about 5 minutes or until mixture thickens slightly. Stir in sage.

3 Drizzle sauce over pork.

Serve with boiled gnocchi, if desired.

plum and soy wok-fried pork

1½ pounds pork tenderloin, thinly sliced

1½ pounds packaged fresh stir-fry vegetables

½ cup plum sauce

2 tablespoons soy sauce

prep + cook time 20 minutes
serves 4

1 Heat oiled wok; stir-fry pork, in batches, until browned. Remove from wok.

2 Stir-fry vegetables in same wok until tender. Return pork to wok with combined sauces; stir-fry until pork is cooked as desired.

roasted pork with apricot relish

2 cans (14 ounces) apricot
   halves in syrup
1¼ pound pork tenderloin
2 tablespoons white vinegar
¼ cup raisins

prep + cook time 30 minutes
serves 4

1 Preheat oven to 475°F (450°F convection).
2 Drain apricots over small bowl. Reserve half
   the juice; chop apricots coarsely.
3 Place pork in oiled baking dish; coat with
   cooking-oil spray. Roast, uncovered, about
   20 minutes or until pork is cooked as desired.
   Cover; stand 5 minutes then slice thickly.
4 Meanwhile, combine apricot, reserved juice,
   vinegar, raisins and ½ cup water in medium
   saucepan; bring to boil. Reduce heat; simmer,
   uncovered, about 20 minutes or until relish
   thickens slightly. Serve pork with relish and
   steamed snow peas, if desired.

chinese barbecued pork

2-pound piece Boston butt
   pork roast
1 cup Chinese barbecue
   (char siu) sauce

prep + cook time 30 minutes
(+ refrigeration)
serves 6

1 Cut pork into quarters lengthways.
2 Combine pork and ⅔ cup sauce in large
   shallow dish; toss to coat. Cover; refrigerate
   3 hours or overnight.
3 Drain pork; discard used marinade. Cook
   pork on heated oiled outoor barbecue grill,
   uncovered, until browned and cooked
   through, brushing with reserved marinade
   during cooking.

roast pork with apricot relish

tip The leanest cuts of pork come from the pork loin, tenderloin, and the leg, trimmed of fat. Pork can dry out if overcooked, so serving it with fruit is an easy way to keep it naturally moist and flavorful.

chinese barbecued pork

tips This is our version of the roasted pork served in Asian restaurants. Serve it with steamed rice and some Asian greens for a main course. There are so many things to do with leftover barbecued pork: add it to soups, fried rice, rice paper rolls and salads.

barbecued pork spareribs with plum and star anise

1 cup plum sauce
⅓ cup oyster sauce
3 star anise
3 pounds pork spareribs

prep + cook time 45 minutes
(plus refrigeration time)
serves 4

1 Combine sauces and star anise in medium saucepan; bring to the boil. Remove from heat; cool 10 minutes.

2 Place pork in large shallow baking dish; brush marinade all over pork. Pour half of marinade over pork, cover; refrigerate 3 hours or overnight, turning pork occasionally. Reserve remaining marinade.

3 Drain pork; discard used marinade. Cook pork in heated oiled grill pan about 30 minutes or until cooked through, turning and brushing frequently with some of the reserved marinade.

4 Boil remaining marinade in small saucepan about 5 minutes or until thickened slightly.

5 Slice spareribs into portions; serve with hot marinade.

tamarind and date pork braise

1¼ pound pork tenderloin, thinly sliced
1 fresh long red chile, finely chopped
2 shallots, thinly sliced
½ cup tamarind and date chutney

prep + cook time 25 minutes
serves 4

1 Cook pork, in batches, in heated oiled large skillet until browned.

2 Add chile and shallot to same skillet; cook, stirring, until shallot is soft.

3 Return pork to the pan with chutney and ⅓ cup water; bring to the boil. Reduce heat; simmer, covered, about 5 minutes or until pork is cooked as desired.

Tamarind and date chutney is available from Indian food stores and some gourmet groceries. You can use your favorite fruit chutney instead.

harissa and lime-rubbed pork

1 lime
½ cup harissa paste
1 clove garlic, crushed
1¼ pounds pork tenderloin

prep + cook time 30 minutes
serves 4

1 Grate zest from lime (you need 2 teaspoons). Juice lime (you need 1 tablespoon).
2 Combine harissa, zest, juice, garlic and pork in large bowl.
3 Cook pork, uncovered, in heated oiled grill pan until browned all over. Cover pork; cook about 10 minutes or until cooked through. Cover pork, stand 5 minutes then slice thickly.

roast peppered pork

1 tablespoon kosher salt
1 tablespoon drained canned green peppercorns in brine, crushed
2 tablespoons mixed dried peppercorns, crushed
2 pound piece pork shoulder

prep + cook time 1 hour 40 minutes
serves 6

1 Combine salt and peppercorns in small bowl.
2 Score pork rind; spray pork with cooking-oil spray. Rub pepper mixture over pork.
3 Cook pork in disposable aluminium baking dish, covered, in outdoor barbecue grill, following manufacturer's instructions, using indirect heat, about 1½ hours or until cooked through.
4 Cover pork; stand 10 minutes then slice.

roast loin of pork

2 sprigs rosemary
5-pound boneless pork loin
  roast, rolled and tied at
  3/4-inch intervals
1 tablespoon olive oil
1 tablespoon kosher salt

prep + cook time 2 hours
(+ standing)
serves 8

1 Preheat oven to 475°F (450°F convection).
2 Tuck the rosemary into the string under the
  pork. Place pork in large baking dish; rub pork
  with oil then salt. Roast about 40 minutes.
  Drain excess fat from dish.
3 Reduce oven to 350°F (325°F convection).
  Roast pork about 1 hour.
4 Transfer pork to plate; cover loosely, stand
  15 minutes before carving.

pork and pancetta kebabs

8 stalks (5 inches) fresh
  rosemary
1¼ pound pork tenderloin,
  cut into 1-inch pieces
8 slices pancetta, halved
1 large red bell pepper,
  cut into 24 pieces

prep + cook time 30 minutes
serves 4

1 Remove leaves from bottom two-thirds of
  each rosemary stalk; reserve 2 tablespoons
  leaves, chop finely. Sharpen trimmed ends of
  stalks to a point.
2 Wrap each piece of pork in one slice of the
  pancetta; thread with bell pepper, alternately,
  onto stalks.
3 Spray kebabs with oil-spray; cook in heated
  oiled grill pan until cooked through.

roast loin of pork

pork and pancetta kebabs

tips Ask your butcher to roll and tie the pork at ¾-inch intervals for you, and to score the skin, if it isn't already done. Apple sauce is delicious with roast pork and crackling. Buy ready-made apple sauce from the supermarket or try making your own by cooking coarsely chopped, peeled apples with a little water in a small saucepan, about 10 minutes or until apple is soft. Stir in sugar and ground cinnamon to taste.

tip Pancetta is an Italian unsmoked bacon. It is pork belly cured in salt and spices then rolled into a sausage shape and dried for several weeks.

Sides

Freshly cooked vegetables and grains add color and texture to your table. A frequently overlooked element because it's so easy to serve the same dishes night after night, these eye-popping sides offer plenty of new ways to liven up a meal.

34

lemon pepper potato wedges

2 pounds potatoes, unpeeled
2 tablespoons olive oil
1 lemon
½ teaspoon freshly ground
   black pepper

prep + cook time 50 minutes
serves 4

1 Preheat oven to 425°F (400°F convection).
   Lightly oil two baking sheets
2 Scrub potatoes; cut into wedges. Toss wedges
   and oil in large bowl. Place wedges, in single
   layer, on baking sheets; roast, uncovered,
   turning occasionally, about 40 minutes or until
   crisp and cooked through.
3 Meanwhile, grate zest from lemon (you
   need 1 tablespoon). Juice lemon (you need
   1 tablespoon). Combine zest, juice and pepper
   in small bowl.
4 Sprinkle lemon pepper all over wedges.

the perfect French fry

2 pounds potatoes
   peanut oil, for deep-frying

prep + cook time 30 minutes
(plus standing time)
serves 4

1 Cut potatoes lengthways into ½-inch-thick
   slices; cut each slice lengthways into ½-inch-
   thick fries. Stand potato in large bowl of cold
   water 30 minutes. Drain; pat dry with paper
   towels.
2 Heat oil in large deep saucepan; cook fries,
   in three batches, about 4 minutes each batch
   or until just tender but not browned. Drain on
   paper towels; stand 10 minutes.
3 Reheat oil; cook fries, in three batches,
   until crisp and golden brown. Drain on paper
   towels. Serve fries sprinkled with sea salt, and
   accompanied with ketchup, if desired.

lemon pepper potato wedges

tip A tasty and attractive side dish, these potato wedges are the perfect accompaniment to meat or fish, served with a crispy green salad.

the perfect French fry

tip Cafes and restaurants around the world use Idaho russet potatoes to make their fries. These potatoes are large and, as the name suggests, they are russet (reddish brown) in color with a white flesh. They are prized for fries because they create dark-colored, caramelized fries.

warm potato and fava beans

10 small potatoes (2½ pounds), thickly sliced
¼ cup French dressing
½ small red onion, thinly sliced
1 pound frozen fava beans

prep + cook time 25 minutes
serve 4

1 Boil, steam or microwave potato until tender; drain.
2 Combine potato in large bowl with dressing and onion.
3 Meanwhile, boil, steam or microwave beans until just tender. Peel; add to potato salad. Toss gently to serve.

paprika potatoes

6 potatoes (2½ pounds), peeled
⅓ cup olive oil
1 tablespoon smoked paprika

prep + cook time 30 minutes
serves 8

1 Boil, steam or microwave potatoes 5 minutes; drain. Slice potatoes thickly. Toss with oil and paprika; cook in heated oiled pan until browned.

blue cheese mash

2 pounds potatoes, coarsely chopped
3 tablespoons butter, softened
3/4 cup hot milk
4 ounces firm blue cheese, crumbled

prep + cook time 30 minutes
serves 6

1 Boil, steam or microwave potato until tender, drain.
2 Mash potato in large bowl with butter and milk until smooth; fold in cheese.

Serve sprinkled with chopped chives, if desired.

batter-fried potato chips

3/4 pound potatoes
3/4 cup self-rising flour
1/2 teaspoon salt
   peanut oil, for deep-frying

prep + cook time 35 minutes
(plus standing time)
serves 6

1 Using sharp knife, mandoline or V-slicer, cut potatoes into 1/8-thick slices. Stand potato in large bowl of cold water 30 minutes. Drain; pat dry with absorbent paper.
2 Meanwhile, place flour and salt in medium bowl; add 1 cup water, whisk until batter is smooth. Dip potato slices, one at a time, in batter.
3 Heat oil in large deep pot; deep-fry potato, in batches, until browned lightly and tender. Drain on absorbent paper.

perfect roast potatoes

6 potatoes (2½ pounds),
  peeled, halved horizontally
2 tablespoons olive oil

prep + cook time 1 hour 10 minutes
serves 4

1 Preheat oven to 425°F (400 °F convection).
  Lightly oil oven tray.
2 Boil, steam or microwave potatoes 5 minutes;
  drain. Pat dry with paper towels; cool 10 minutes.
3 Gently rake rounded sides of potatoes with tines
  of fork; place potatoes in single layer, cut-side
  down, on baking sheet. Brush with oil; roast,
  uncovered, in oven about 50 minutes or until
  potatoes are browned and crisp.

potatoes anna

2½ pounds potatoes, peeled
  4 tablespoons butter, melted

prep + cook time 1 hour 10 minutes
serves 6

1 Preheat oven to 475°F (450°F convection).
  Lightly oil shallow 8-cup (10-inch) round
  ovenproof baking dish.
2 Using sharp knife, mandoline or V-slicer, slice
  potatoes into ⅛-inch slices; pat dry with
  paper towels. Place a single layer of potato,
  slightly overlapping, into baking dish; brush
  with a little of the butter. Continue layering
  remaining potato and butter, cover dish with
  foil; bake 20 minutes.
3 Remove foil; use metal spatula to press down
  on potato.
4 Reduce oven temperature to 425°F (400°F
  convection); bake about 30 minutes or until
  top is crisp and browned lightly. Cut into
  wedges to serve.

perfect roast potatoes

potatoes anna

tip Perfectly roasted potatoes should be crisp and golden brown on the outside, fluffy and moist on the inside. Olive oil is better to brush potatoes with than any other oil or butter because it tolerates high oven temperatures and lends its pleasant taste to the potatoes. Gently raking along the length of the peeled potato surface with the tines of a fork assists in crisping. Don't crowd potatoes on the baking sheet because they will brown unevenly.

tips In the late 1800s, French chef Adolphe Dugléré devised this dish in honor of Anna Deslions, a courtesan who entertained clients in a private dining room within his restaurant. Pressing down on the potato during the cooking process compacts it and makes it easier to slice.

potato skins with horseradish cream

2 pounds potatoes, unpeeled
¼ cup prepared horseradish
¾ cup light sour cream
¼ teaspoon smoked paprika

prep + cook time 1 hour 15 minutes
serves 4

1 Preheat oven to 425°F (400°F convection).
2 Scrub potatoes; coat with cooking-oil spray and prick skins with a fork. Place potatoes on baking sheet; bake, uncovered, about 50 minutes or until tender. Cool 10 minutes.
3 Cut each potato into six wedges; carefully remove flesh (save for another use), leaving skins intact. Place potato skins, skin-side down, on wire rack over oven tray; coat with cooking-oil spray. Roast, uncovered, about 20 minutes or until crisp.
4 Meanwhile, combine horseradish cream, sour cream and paprika in small bowl.
5 Serve skins with horseradish cream.

cottage fries

2 pounds potatoes
2 tablespoons butter, chopped
½ cup vegetable oil
1 onion, thickly sliced

prep + cook time 20 minutes
(plus standing time)
serves 4

1 Using sharp knife, mandoline or V-slicer, slice potatoes into ⅛-inch slices. Soak potato in large bowl of cold water 30 minutes. Drain; pat dry with paper towels.
2 Heat a third of the butter and a third of the oil in large deep skillet; cook a third of the potato and a third of the onion, stirring occasionally, until browned lightly and cooked through. Drain on paper towels; cover to keep warm.
3 Repeat step 2, in two batches. Return cottage fries to skillet; toss to heat through. Season with freshly cracked black pepper and salt, if desired.

hasselback potatoes

4 large Idaho potatoes,
  halved horizontally
2 tablespoons olive oil
¼ cup packaged breadcrumbs
½ cup finely grated Cheddar
  cheese

prep + cook time 1 hour 20 minutes
serves 4

1 Preheat oven to 375°F (350°F convection).
2 Place one potato half, cut-side down, on chopping board; place a chopstick along each side of potato. Slice potato thinly, cutting through to chopsticks to prevent cutting all the way through. Repeat with remaining potato.
3 Coat potato in half the oil in medium baking dish; place, rounded-side up, in a single layer. Roast, uncovered, 45 minutes, brushing with remaining oil. Continue roasting without brushing about 15 minutes or until potatoes are cooked through.
4 Sprinkle combined breadcrumbs and cheese over potatoes; roast, uncovered, 10 minutes or until topping is lightly browned.

squash gratin

3 pounds butternut squash
4 cloves garlic, halved
½ cup heavy cream
⅔ cup grated Parmesan cheese

prep + cook time 1 hour
serves 8

1 Preheat oven to 400°F (375·F convection). Coat an 8-cup gratin dish with cooking spray.
2 Peel squash, remove seeds; chop into evenly sized pieces. Place squash in dish with garlic; roast about 25 minutes or until squash is almost cooked through.
3 Pour cream over squash; sprinkle with cheese. Cook another 25 minutes or until squash is tender.

duchesse potatoes

2 pounds potatoes, peeled, coarsely chopped

3 egg yolks

4 tablespoons butter, melted

prep + cook time 1 hour
makes 40

1 Preheat oven to 350°F (325°F convection); oil and line baking sheets with parchment paper.

2 Boil, steam or microwave potato until tender; drain. Mash potato in large bowl with egg yolks and butter.

3 Spoon potato mixture into large piping bag fitted with a ½-inch fluted tip; pipe potato into 1-inch rosette-shaped swirls onto baking sheets.

4 Bake about 30 minutes or until lightly browned.

balsamic-roasted potatoes

3 pounds baby new potatoes, halved

2 tablespoons butter, melted

¼ cup balsamic vinegar

prep + cook time 1 hour 20 minutes
serves 6

1 Preheat oven to 325°F (300·F convection).

2 Combine potato, butter and vinegar in medium baking dish. Roast, uncovered, brushing occasionally with the vinegar mixture about 1¼ hours or until potatoes are tender and lightly browned.

duchesse potatoes

balsamic-roasted potatoes

tips For a variation, stir ½ cup grated Parmesan cheese into the potato mixture before piping. The potato can be piped up to 3 hours ahead; keep, covered, in the refrigerator.

tip Try stirring a large handful of baby spinach into potato mixture just before serving.

broccolini with honey

1½ pounds broccolini, halved
   crossways
1 tablespoon light soy sauce
2 teaspoons honey
2 teaspoons toasted sesame
   seeds

prep + cook time 10 minutes
serves 4

1 Cook broccolini in large parchment paper-lined steamer, over large saucepan of simmering water, about 5 minutes or until tender.
2 Meanwhile, combine sauce, honey and 1 tablespoon boiling water in small bowl.
3 Serve broccolini drizzled with sauce; sprinkle with sesame seeds.

broccoli polonaise

2 tablespoons butter, melted
½ cup stale breadcrumbs
2 hard-boiled eggs, finely
   chopped
¾ pound broccoli

prep + cook time 20 minutes
serves 4

1 Heat half the butter in large skillet; cook breadcrumbs, stirring, until browned and crisp. Combine breadcrumbs in small bowl with egg.
2 Boil, steam or microwave broccoli until just tender; drain.
3 Top broccoli with polonaise mixture then drizzle with the remaining melted butter.

broccolini with honey

tip Broccolini is the product of a naturally occurring romance between broccoli and an Asian vegetable called gai-lan—not the result of genetic modification. Choose broccolini with shiny stems and dark green buds and leaves.

broccoli polonaise

tip A "polonaise" is the French interpretation of a classic Polish style of presenting cooked vegetables such as broccoli, cauliflower, asparagus and the like, by topping them with chopped hard-boiled egg, buttered breadcrumbs and chopped parsley.

grilled corn, fava beans and bell pepper

2   trimmed ears of corn
½   pound frozen fava beans,
    thawed, peeled
1   small red bell pepper,
    finely chopped
2   teaspoons butter

prep + cook time 30 minutes
serves 4

1 Cook corn in heated oiled grill pan until just tender. When cool enough to handle, use sharp knife to cut kernels from cobs.
2 Meanwhile, boil, steam or microwave fava beans until tender; drain.
3 Place corn and beans in large bowl with bell pepper and butter; toss gently to combine.

baby carrots with orange maple syrup

1½ pounds baby carrots
1   large orange
2   tablespoons butter
1   tablespoon maple syrup

prep + cook time 35 minutes
serves 4

1 Boil, steam or microwave carrots until just tender.
2 Meanwhile, grate zest from orange (you need 1 teaspoon). Juice orange (you need 1 tablespoon.)
3 Melt butter in heated large skillet, add zest, juice and syrup; cook, stirring, until mixture boils. Reduce heat; simmer, uncovered, until syrup mixture thickens slightly. Add drained carrots to pan; stir gently to coat in orange maple syrup.

creamed mint peas

1 pound frozen peas
2 cloves garlic, unpeeled
½ cup plain yogurt
½ cup fresh mint

prep + cook time 15 minutes
serves 4

1 Cook peas and garlic in saucepan of boiling water until peas soften; drain.
2 Peel garlic; blend or process garlic, peas, yogurt and mint until smooth.

fresh peas, caraway and parmesan

4 tablespoons butter
1 teaspoon caraway seeds
4 cups fresh peas (640g)
½ cup grated Parmesan cheese

prep + cook time 25 minutes
serves 4

1 Melt butter in heated large skillet; cook seeds, stirring, until fragrant.
2 Add peas to pan; cook, stirring, until peas are just tender. Serve peas sprinkled with cheese.

peas with mint butter

2¼ cups fresh shelled peas

1 tablespoon butter, softened

1 tablespoon finely chopped fresh mint

1 teaspoon fresh lemon zest

prep + cook time 10 minutes
serves 4

1 Boil, steam or microwave peas until just tender; drain.
2 Meanwhile, combine remaining ingredients in small bowl.
3 Serve peas topped with butter mixture.

sesame patty-pan squash and sugar snap peas

8 yellow patty-pan squash (about ½ pound)

¼ pound sugar snap peas, trimmed

2 teaspoons soy sauce

2 teaspoons toasted sesame seeds

prep + cook time 15 minutes
serves 4

1 Boil, steam or microwave squash and peas, separately, until tender; drain.
2 Place vegetables in large bowl with remaining ingredients; toss gently to combine.

peas with mint butter

tip You need approximately 2 pounds fresh pea pods to get the required amount of shelled peas needed for this recipe. You could also use frozen peas.

sesame patty-pan squash and sugar snap peas

tip Sugar snap peas are very similar to snow peas, but they have rounder pods. As the name suggests, sugar snap peas are sweet, crunchy and juicy.

asparagus with anchovies

¾ pound asparagus, trimmed
⅓ cup extra virgin olive oil
2 cloves garlic, thinly sliced
6 anchovy fillets, drained,
  coarsely chopped

prep + cook time 10 minutes
serves 8

1 Preheat oven to 400°F (375°F convection).
2 Place asparagus in shallow baking dish;
  pour over combined oil, garlic and anchovies.
  Toss asparagus to coat in the oil mixture.
3 Roast about 5 minutes or until asparagus
  is just tender.

*If buying a day or two in advance, store
asparagus upright in the fridge with cut ends in
water and plastic wrap draped over the tips and
secured to the container with a rubber band.*

asparagus with tomato dressing

¾ pound asparagus, trimmed
⅓ cup extra virgin olive oil
2 tablespoons balsamic vinegar
2 tomatoes, peeled, seeded,
  finely chopped

prep + cook time 10 minutes
serves 4

1 Cook asparagus in heated, lightly oiled grill
  pan about 5 minutes or until tender.
2 Serve topped with combined oil, vinegar
  and tomato.

*Serve sprinkled with small basil leaves if desired.
To peel tomatoes, cut a small cross at the base
of the tomato. Plunge in boiling water for
20 seconds until skin cracks. Remove with slotted
spoon and cool in iced water. Slip the skin off
with a small knife.*

pan-fried asparagus
with parmesan

1 tablespoon olive oil
1 pound asparagus, trimmed
½ cup flaked Parmesan cheese
½ teaspoon fresh black pepper

prep + cook time 10 minutes
serves 4

1 Heat oil in large skillet; cook asparagus, in batches, if necessary, until just tender.
2 Serve asparagus sprinkled with cheese and black pepper.

prosciutto and cheese asparagus

¾ pound asparagus, trimmed
¼ prosciutto
4 ounces fontina cheese, cut into 10 sticks

prep + cook time 15 minutes
makes 10

1 Top each prosciutto slice with cheese; wrap around asparagus spears.
2 Grill until prosciutto is crisp.

prosciutto-wrapped bean bundles

1 pound mixed yellow and
  green beans, trimmed
8 slices prosciutto
2 tablespoons butter
1 tablespoon rinsed, drained
  baby capers

prep + cook time 30 minutes
serves 8

1 Cook beans in medium saucepan of boiling
  water until just tender. Rinse under cold
  water; drain. Divide beans into eight equal
  bundles.
2 Place one slice of prosciutto on board; top
  with one bundle of beans. Wrap prosciutto
  over beans; continue rolling to enclose beans
  tightly. Repeat with remaining prosciutto
  and beans.
3 Cook bean bundles in heated oiled large skillet
  until prosciutto is crisp. Remove from skillet;
  cover to keep warm.
4 Melt butter in same pan; cook capers, stirring,
  1 minute. Serve bean bundles drizzled with
  caper mixture.

green beans almondine

3/4 pound green beans
1 tablespoon butter
2 slices center-cut bacon
1/4 cup slivered almonds

prep + cook time 15 minutes
serves 4

1 Boil, steam or microwave beans until just
  tender; drain. Rinse under cold water; drain.
2 Melt butter in heated large skillet; cook bacon
  and nuts, stirring, until bacon is crisp. Add
  beans; stir until hot.

prosciutto-wrapped bean bundles

tip These delicious salty bundles are also fantastic with a squeeze of lemon and a sprinkle of chopped parsley.

green beans almondine

tip For a vegetarian option, substitute cubed tofu, tempeh or eggplant for the bacon.

beans, tomatoes and hazelnuts

3/4 cup roasted hazelnuts, skinned, coarsely chopped

1/2 cup mustard dressing

3/4 pound green beans, trimmed

3/4 cup cherry tomatoes, halved

1 Combine nuts and dressing in small bowl.

2 Boil, steam or microwave beans until tender; drain. Rinse under cold water; drain.

3 Combine beans, tomato and dressing mixture in medium bowl; toss gently.

prep + cook time 20 minutes
serves 4

tomato and red onion salad

4 tomatoes, thinly sliced

2 red onions, thinly sliced

2 tablespoons red wine vinegar

1 tablespoon olive oil

1 Arrange tomato and onion on serving platter; drizzle with vinegar and oil. Season to taste.

prep time 10 minutes
serves 6

beans, tomatoes and hazelnuts

tip To remove skins from hazelnuts, wrap the toasted nuts in a clean tea-towel and gently rub until skins come away.

tomato and red onion salad

tips This salad is the perfect accompaniment for barbecued steaks or fish. Be sure to use ripe, deep red tomatoes for this recipe.

bell pepper and haloumi

- 3 small bell peppers
- 8 ounces haloumi cheese, cut into ½-inch slices
- 2 tablespoons olive oil
- 1 tablespoon lemon juice

prep + cook time 50 minutes
serves 6

1 Preheat oven to 400°F (375°F convection).
2 Quarter bell peppers; discard seeds and membranes. Brush bell peppers and cheese with half of the oil; cook, in batches, in heated grill until both are lightly browned and bell pepper is tender.
3 Cut cheese into even-sized pieces; cut each bell pepper into even-sized pieces.
4 Place cheese and pepper pieces, in single layer, on large oven tray; pour combined juice and remaining oil over mixture. Season with pepper. Roast, uncovered, in oven about 5 minutes or until hot.

Serve immediately as haloumi tends to become chewy when it cools down. There are several varieties of haloumi available: 100% cow's milk or a mix of sheep's and goat's milk.

spinach, chorizo and chickpeas

- 2 hard chorizo sausages (5 ounces each), thinly sliced
- 5 ounces baby spinach
- 1 can (15 ounces) chickpeas, rinsed, drained
- 1 tablespoon red wine vinegar

prep + cook time 10 minutes
serves 6

1 Cook chorizo in heated large skillet until browned both sides. Drain on paper towels. Add spinach to same pan; cook, uncovered, until wilted.
2 Place spinach, chickpeas, vinegar and chorizo in large bowl; toss gently.

roasted caramelized parsnips

3 pounds parsnips, halved
  lengthways
¼ cup olive oil
⅓ cup light brown sugar
1 tablespoon finely chopped
  fresh flat-leaf parsley

1 Preheat oven to 425°F (400°F convection).
2 Combine parsnip, oil and sugar in large baking
  dish; roast about 1 hour or until parsnip is
  browned and tender.
3 Serve parsnip sprinkled with parsley.

prep + cook time 1 hour 10 minutes
serves 6

mustard and honey-glazed sweet potato

2 pounds sweet potato,
  unpeeled
⅓ cup honey
2 tablespoons wholegrain
  mustard
1 tablespoon coarsely chopped
  fresh rosemary

1 Preheat oven to 425°F (400°F convection).
2 Halve sweet potato lengthways; cut each half
  into 1-inch wedges.
3 Combine remaining ingredients in large
  bowl, add sweet potato; toss sweet potato to
  coat in mixture. Place sweet potato mixture
  in large shallow baking dish. Roast, uncovered,
  about 1 hour or until sweet potato is tender
  and slightly caramelized.

prep + cook time 1 hour 10 minutes
serves 4

rosemary and garlic wedges

2 pounds Yukon gold potatoes,
  unpeeled, cut into wedges

6 rosemary sprigs, chopped

2 tablespoons olive oil

2 cloves garlic, crushed

prep + cook time 50 minutes
serves 6

1 Preheat oven to 400°F (425°F convection).

2 Combine potato in large bowl with rosemary,
  oil and garlic. Roast wedges on rimmed baking
  sheet about 40 minutes or until tender.

creamed spinach

3 tablespoons butter

2½ pounds spinach, trimmed

1 cup heavy cream

prep + cook time 25 minutes
serves 8

1 Melt butter in large skillet; cook spinach,
  stirring, until wilted.

2 Add cream; bring to the boil. Reduce heat;
  simmer, uncovered, until liquid reduces by
  half. Season to taste.

rosemary and garlic wedges

tip Yukon gold potatoes have firm yellow flesh and are perfect for roasting. Give them a good scrub and eat them with their skin on.

creamed spinach

tips Always wash spinach thoroughly before using to remove any grit. You will need about four bunches of spinach for this recipe.

spinach mash

3 pounds potatoes, peeled, coarsely chopped

10 ounces spinach, stems removed

4 tablespoons butter, softened

3/4 cup heavy cream, heated

prep + cook time 30 minutes
serves 6

1 Boil, steam or microwave potato until tender; drain.

2 Meanwhile, boil, steam or microwave spinach until wilted; drain. Squeeze out excess liquid. Blend or process spinach with butter until almost smooth.

3 Mash potato in large bowl; stir in cream and spinach mixture.

fava bean mash

2 pounds fresh fava beans

1/3 cup heavy cream, heated

2 pounds potatoes, peeled, coarsely chopped

3 tablespoons butter melted

prep + cook time 30 minutes
serves 4

1 Shell beans; discard pods. Boil, steam or microwave beans until just tender; drain. Peel away gray-colored outer shells; blend or process beans until smooth. Stir in 2 tablespoons of the cream.

2 Boil, steam or microwave potato until tender; drain. Mash potato in large bowl; stir in mashed bean mixture, butter and remaining cream.

tip For a Greek flavor add some crumbled feta cheese, lemon zest and juice. You will need about two bunches of spinach for this recipe.

spinach mash

tips Peeling fava beans is a pain but it's well worth the effort when you see their bright color. If you can't get fresh fava beans use 8 ounces frozen beans—you will still need to boil the beans and peel away the gray shells.

fava bean mash

cauliflower puree

1½ pounds cauliflower, coarsely chopped
 2 tablespoons butter
 ¼ cup heavy cream
 12 tablespoon lemon juice

prep + cook time 20 minutes
serves 4

1 Boil, steam or microwave cauliflower until tender; drain.
2 Mash cauliflower with butter, cream and juice in large bowl until smooth.

sweet potato and carrot mash

 2 sweet potatoes, coarsely chopped
 2 carrots, coarsely chopped
 1 teaspoon ground cumin
 ⅓ cup buttermilk

prep + cook time 30 minutes
serves 8

1 Boil, steam or microwave sweet potato and carrot, separately, until tender; drain.
2 Toast cumin in small dry skillet over medium-high heat until fragrant. Mash vegetables in large bowl with cumin and buttermilk until smooth.

sweet potato mash

1 pound potatoes, coarsely chopped

1 pound sweet potatoes, peeled, coarsely chopped

¼ cup hot chicken stock

2 tablespoons butter, softened

prep + cook time 25 minutes
serves 4

1 Boil, steam or microwave potato and sweet potato, together, until tender; drain.

2 Mash potato and sweet potato in large bowl; stir in stock and butter.

butternut mash

1 pound potatoes, coarsely chopped

1 pound peeled and seeded butternut squash, coarsely chopped

2 tablespoons butter, softened

1 teaspoon ground cumin

prep + cook time 30 minutes
serves 4

1 Boil, steam or microwave potato and butternut squash, together, until tender; drain.

2 Mash potato and butternut squash in large bowl; stir in butter and cumin.

fennel mash

4 tablespoons butter

1 large fennel bulb, thinly sliced

2 pounds potatoes, peeled, coarsely chopped

½ cup heavy cream, heated

prep + cook time 30 minutes
serves 4

1 Melt butter in large skillet; cook fennel, covered about 10 minutes or until very soft. Blend or process fennel until smooth.

2 Meanwhile, boil, steam or microwave potato until tender; drain. Mash potato in large bowl; stir in fennel and cream.

celeriac purée

2 cups chicken stock

2 pounds celeriac, trimmed, peeled, coarsely chopped

½ cup (125ml) cream

1 tablespoon finely chopped fresh chives

prep + cook time 35 minutes
serves 4

1 Bring stock to the boil in medium saucepan; add celeriac, return to a boil. Reduce heat; simmer, covered, about 30 minutes or until celeriac is tender. Drain.

2 Stand celeriac 10 minutes, then blend or process, in batches, with cream until smooth. Serve sprinkled with chives.

fennel mash

celeriac purée

tip For a Greek flavor add some crumbled feta cheese, lemon zest and juice. You will need about two bunches of spinach for this recipe.

tip Celeriac is a member of the celery family, though it is the root that is used, not the stalks as with celery. It has an earthy and pungent celery-like flavor and a creamy texture. It can be grated and eaten raw in salads, or boiled and mashed or puréed like potatoes.

balsamic-glazed baby onions

1 tablespoon balsamic vinegar
1 tablespoon wholegrain
   mustard
¼ cup honey
1 pound baby onions, halved

prep + cook time 25 minutes
serves 8

1 Combine vinegar, mustard and honey in
  small saucepan; bring to the boil. Simmer,
  uncovered, about 5 minutes or until glaze
  thickens.
2 Cook onion in heated oiled large skillet,
  brushing constantly with glaze, stirring,
  until browned and cooked as desired.

roasted mushrooms with ricotta

4 portabello mushrooms
   (about ¾ pound), stems
   removed
½ cup ricotta cheese
2 tablespoons coarsely
   chopped fresh flat-leaf
   parsley
2 scallions, finely chopped

prep + cook time 15 minutes
serves 2

1 Preheat oven to 400°F (375°F convection).
2 Place mushrooms, stem-side up, on oven tray.
  Roast, uncovered, about 15 minutes.
3 Meanwhile, combine remaining ingredients
  in small bowl.
4 Serve mushrooms topped with cheese mixture.

balsamic-glazed baby onions

tip Baby onions, often called pickling onions, are just immature cooking onions. They have a delicate sweet flavor and are excellent served with meat or added to salads.

roasted mushrooms with ricotta

tip Portabellos are large, flat mushrooms that have a rich earthy, full-bodied flavor and meaty texture, making them perfect for roasting grilling.

steamed lemon jasmine rice

1 cup jasmine rice
1½ cups chicken stock
2 teaspoons fresh lemon zest
¼ cup finely chopped fresh
   chives

prep + cook time 25 minutes
serves 4

1 Combine rice, stock and ½ cup water in large saucepan; bring to a boil. Reduce heat; simmer, covered tightly, about 10 minutes or until rice is cooked.
2 Remove from heat; stand, covered, 5 minutes. Stir in zest and chives.

yellow coconut rice

1¾ cups white long-grain rice
1 can (12 ounces) coconut
   cream
½ teaspoon ground turmeric
   pinch saffron threads

prep + cook time
20 minutes (plus standing time)
serves 4

1 Stand rice in large bowl of cold water 30 minutes. Drain rice; rinse under cold water until water runs clear. Drain.
2 Place rice and remaining ingredients with 1¼ cups water in large heavy saucepan; cover, bring to a boil, stirring occasionally. Reduce heat; simmer, covered, about 15 minutes or until rice is tender. Remove from heat; stand, covered, 5 minutes before serving.

spinach couscous

1½ cups couscous
1 tablespoon butter
1 cup baby spinach,
  thinly sliced

prep time 10 minutes
serves 4

1 Combine couscous with 1½ cups boiling water
  in large heatproof bowl, cover; stand about
  5 minutes or until liquid is absorbed, fluffing
  with fork occasionally.
2 Stir butter and spinach into couscous.

date and pine nut couscous

½ cup pine nuts
2 cups couscous
8 dried dates, thinly sliced
2 tablespoons coarsely
  chopped fresh cilantro

prep time 10 minutes
serves 4

1 Toast pine nuts in a small dry skillet over
  medium high heat until fragrant.
2 Combine couscous with 2 cups boiling water
  in large heatproof bowl, cover; stand about
  5 minutes or until liquid is absorbed, fluffing
  with fork occasionally.
3 Stir dates, nuts and coriander into couscous.

green rice

1 cup jasmine rice
1²/₃ cups canned coconut milk
2 fresh long green chiles, thinly sliced
1 teaspoon fresh lime zest

prep + cook time 25 minutes
serves 4

1 Rinse rice under cold water until water runs clear; drain.
2 Combine rice with coconut milk, ⅓ cup of water, chiles and zest in medium heavy-based saucepan; bring to a boil, stirring occasionally. Reduce heat; simmer, covered tightly, about 15 minutes or until rice is tender. Remove from heat; stand, covered, 5 minutes.

parsley and almond pilaf

¼ cup sliced almonds
1 tablespoon butter
1 cup basmati rice
¼ cup coarsely chopped fresh flat-leaf parsley

prep + cook time 25 minutes
serves 4

1 Toast almonds in a small, dry skillet over medium-high heat until fragrant.
2 Melt butter in medium saucepan; cook rice, stirring, 1 minute. Add 2 cups of water; bring to a boil. Reduce heat; simmer, covered, about 20 minutes or until rice is just tender.
3 Remove from heat; fluff rice with fork. Stir in parsley and almonds.

This cooking method is very popular in Greece and India. You can easily make it a quick meal by adding meat and chopped vegetables.

cumin couscous

1 cup couscous
1 tablespoon olive oil
1 teaspoon ground cumin

prep + cook time 10 minutes
serves 4

1 Combine couscous and 1 cup of boiling water in large heatproof bowl, cover; stand about 5 minutes or until liquid is absorbed, fluffing with fork occasionally. Add oil and cumin; toss gently to combine.

grilled parmesan polenta

1 cup polenta
1 tablespoon butter, chopped
1 cup grated Parmesan cheese

prep + cook time 25 minutes
(+ refrigeration)
serves 4

1 Coat a deep 8-inch square cake pan with cooking oil.
2 Bring 4 cups of water to a boil in large saucepan. Gradually stir in polenta; simmer, stirring, about 10 minutes or until polenta thickens. Stir in butter and cheese.
3 Spread polenta into cake pan; cool 10 minutes. Cover; refrigerate 3 hours or until firm.
4 Turn polenta onto board. Cut polenta into four squares; cut squares into triangles. Cook polenta, both sides, in heated oiled grill pan until browned and heated through.

Stovetop Desserts

Some consider dessert the most important part of the meal, and these recipes prove you don't need a long list of ingredients or hours of preparation to create sweet and sumptuous desserts.

34

fudge sauce

6 ounces semisweet chocolate chips
1 tablespoon butter
¼ teaspoon vanilla extract
½ cup heavy cream

prep + cook time 15 minutes
makes 1 cup

1 Place chocolate and butter in small heatproof bowl set over small saucepan of simmering water (do not allow water to touch base of bowl). Stir until chocolate is melted. Add extract and cream; stir until combined. Serve sauce warm.

Sauce goes well with ice cream, puddings, mousse and poached fruit.

crème anglaise

1 vanilla bean, halved lengthways
1½ cups milk
⅓ cup sugar
4 egg yolks

prep + cook time
30 minutes (plus refrigeration time)
makes 1½ cups

1 Scrape vanilla bean seeds into medium saucepan; add pod, milk and one tablespoon of the sugar. Bring to a boil then strain into large glass measuring cup. Discard pod.

2 Meanwhile, combine egg yolks and remaining sugar in medium heatproof bowl set over medium saucepan of simmering water (do not allow water to touch base of bowl). Whisk until mixture is thick and creamy then gradually whisk in the hot milk mixture.
3 Return custard mixture to pan; stir over low heat until mixture is just thick enough to coat the back of a spoon.
4 Return custard to bowl; refrigerate about 1 hour or until cold.

Sauce goes well with apple pie, poached plums, chocolate cake and fresh figs.

fudge sauce

crème anglaise

caramel fondue with fresh fruit

½ cup firmly packed brown
   sugar
⅔ cup heavy cream
4 tablespoons butter
   fresh fruit, to serve

prep + cook time 10 minutes
serves 4

1 Combine sugar, cream and butter in small
saucepan. Cook, stirring, until sugar dissolves
and butter melts; bring to a boil. Reduce heat;
simmer, uncovered, 3 minutes.
2 Remove from heat; cool 10 minutes before
serving with fruit.

*We used strawberries, bananas and pears, you
can use any combination of fruit you like.*

balsamic strawberries with mascarpone

1 pound strawberries, halved
¼ cup sugar
2 tablespoons balsamic vinegar
1 cup mascarpone cheese

prep + cook time 5 minutes
(+ refrigeration)
serves 4

1 Combine strawberries, sugar and vinegar in
medium bowl, cover; refrigerate 20 minutes.
2 Serve strawberries with mascarpone; drizzle
with juices from bowl.

Serve with chopped mint or basil leaves.

tip We used bananas, strawberries and pears, but try any combination of fruit you like. This recipe makes 1 cup sauce, which freezes nicely if you happen to have any leftovers

caramel fondue with fresh fruit

tip Strawberries and balsamic vinegar are a food match made in heaven. The rich, sweet and complex flavor of the vinegar brings out the intense sweetness of the strawberries. Topped with mascarpone cheese, dessert doesn't get much better than this.

balsamic strawberries with mascarpone

choc-cherry mascarpone

1 can (15 ounces) sour cherries
  in syrup
1¼ cup heavy cream
6 ounces semisweet chocolate
  chips
8 ounces mascarpone cheese

prep + cook time 15 minutes
(plus cooling and refrigeration time)
serves 6

1 Drain cherries, reserve ¼ cup of syrup.
2 Combine cream and reserved syrup in medium
  saucepan; bring to a boil. Remove from heat;
  add chocolate, stir until smooth. Cool.
3 Beat cheese and chocolate mixture in small
  bowl with electric mixer until smooth.
4 Divide cherries between six ¾-cup dishes;
  top with chocolate mixture. Refrigerate about
  30 minutes or until set.

peaches with creamy yogurt

2 jars (28 ounces each)
  canned peaches
2 cinnamon sticks
2 cups vanilla yogurt

prep + cook time 15 minutes
serves 6

1 Drain the juice from peaches into medium
  saucepan; add cinnamon to the pan. Bring to
  a boil; reduce heat, simmer, uncovered, 3
  minutes. Remove from heat. Add peaches to
  juice mixture;
  cover pan, stand 10 minutes before serving.
2 Spoon warm peaches and a little of the juice
  into serving bowls; serve with yogurt.

plums with sour cream

1 jar (28 ounces) plums in
   syrup, drained
½ cup sour cream
½ cup honey-flavored yogurt
⅓ cup firmly packed brown
   sugar

prep + cook time 10 minutes
serves 4

1 Halve plums; discard pits. Divide plums among
   four 1-cup shallow ovenproof serving dishes.
2 Preheat broiler.
3 Combine sour cream, yogurt and 2 tablespoons
   of the sugar in small bowl. Spoon sour cream
   mixture over plums; sprinkle with remaining
   sugar. Place under broiler about 3 minutes or
   until sugar dissolves.

pears with choc-mint sauce

6 ounces peppermint cream
   dark chocolate, coarsely
   chopped
¼ cup heavy cream
1 jar (28 ounces) pear halves
   in natural juice, drained
4 mint chocolate cookies,
   finely chopped

prep + cook time 10 minutes
serves 4

1 Melt chocolate with cream in medium
   heatproof bowl set over medium saucepan
   of simmering water (do not let water touch
   base of bowl).
2 Divide pears among serving dishes; drizzle
   with sauce then sprinkle with cookie crumbs.
   Serve with ice cream, if desired.

white chocolate and black cherry rice pudding

6 cups milk

²/₃ cup arborio rice

¼ pound (4 ounces) white chocolate, finely chopped

1 can (15 ounces) pitted black cherries, drained

prep + cook time 55 minutes
serves 6

1 Combine milk, rice and half the chocolate in medium saucepan; bring to a boil. Reduce heat; simmer over very low heat, stirring often, about 40 minutes or until rice is tender.

2 Serve rice warm, topped with cherries and remaining chocolate. Sprinkle with nutmeg, if desired.

apple and blackberry gelatin

1 packet (3 ounces) blackcurrant gelatin

1 cup frozen blackberries

1 apple, peeled, cored, finely chopped

½ cup whipped cream

prep + cook time 10 minutes
(plus refrigeration time)
serves 4

1 Make gelatin according to directions on package.

2 Divide blackberries and apple among four ¾-cup glasses; pour gelatin over top. Refrigerate about 3 hours or until jelly has set.

3 Beat cream in small bowl with electric mixer until soft peaks form. Serve topped with whipped cream.

white chocolate and black cherry rice pudding

apple and blackberry gelatin

tip Cooking the milk, rice and white chocolate together gives this dessert a luxurious, velvety texture that is perfectly offset by the sweet tartness of the black cherries.

tip These gelatins are so simple to make, and yet they create such an impressive-looking dessert, especially when served in sophisticated glassware. Make them ahead of time and take the stress out of your dinner party.

peach melba

4 peaches

½ pound fresh or thawed frozen raspberries

1 tablespoon confectioners' sugar, approximately

2 cups vanilla ice cream

prep + cook time 10 minutes (plus cooling time)
serves 4

1 Place 4 cups water in medium saucepan; bring to a boil. Add peaches; simmer, uncovered, 5 minutes. Remove peaches; place in bowl of cold water. When peaches are cold, remove skins.

2 Meanwhile, push raspberries through fine sieve into small bowl; sweeten pulp with confectioners' sugar to taste.

3 Serve peach halves with ice-cream; top with sauce, and extra raspberries, if desired.

fresh peaches with mint

6 peaches

¼ cup loosely packed fresh mint

2 tablespoons lemon juice

1 tablespoon honey

prep time 10 minutes (+ standing)
serves 6

1 Halve and pit peaches; cut into wedges and place in serving bowl. Sprinkle with mint; drizzle with combined juice and honey.

2 Stand at room temperature 30 minutes before serving.

Serve with Greek-style yogurt, if desired.

peach melba

tip Peach Melba was created more than a century ago by famed French chef August Escoffier at the Savoy Hotel in London, in honor of the Australian soprano Dame Nellie Melba (1861–1931). Dame Nellie reportedly loved ice cream but ate it rarely for fear that it would hurt her vocal chords.

fresh peaches with mint

tip Peaches have a short season but you can make this dessert with mixed fresh berries, mango, watermelon or honeydew melon.

honeyed bananas with lime

2 limes
2 tablespoons honey
4 large bananas, thickly sliced
12 small scoops coconut ice cream

prep + cook time 10 minutes
serves 6

1 Peel ½-inch wide strips of zest from limes. Squeeze limes (you need 2 tablespoons of juice).
2 Combine zest in medium skillet with juice and honey; stir over low heat until honey softens. Remove skillet from heat; remove zest and shred finely.
3 Add banana to honey mixture; toss gently. Divide banana mixture among serving bowls; serve with scoops of vanilla ice cream and shredded lime zest.

sweet lime mangoes

4 mangoes
1 lime
2 tablespoons light brown sugar
½ cup yogurt.

prep + cook time 15 minutes
serves 4

1 Preheat broiler.
2 Slice cheeks from mangoes; score each in shallow criss-cross pattern. Place scored-side-up on baking sheet.
3 Finely grate 2 teaspoons zest from lime. Squeeze juice from lime (you need 1 tablespoon juice). Combine zest, juice and sugar in small bowl; drizzle over mango.
4 Broil until sugar caramelizes; serve with yogurt.

honeyed bananas with lime

tip If you have some shredded coconut in the pantry toast a little in a dry skillet, stirring, until lightly browned and sprinkle over the bananas just before serving for a bit of crunch.

sweet lime mangoes

tip Line the baking sheet with aluminum foil to prevent the sugar from burning onto the sheet. This will make cleaning up much easier.

tropical fruit skewers with orange glaze

*We used strawberries, bananas,
pineapple and kiwifruit in this recipe.
Use any tropical fruit you like.*

1 large orange
2 tablespoons brown sugar
4 cups chopped mixed
    tropical fruit
6 ounces honey-flavored
    yogurt

prep + cook time 35 minutes
serves 4

1 Grate zest from orange (you need 1 teaspoon).
  Juice orange (you need ¼ cup). Combine zest,
  juice and sugar in small saucepan; stir over
  low heat until sugar dissolves. Cool.
2 Thread fruits, alternately, onto skewers. Brush
  orange mixture over skewers..
3 Grill skewers in a lightly oiled grill pan, turning
  occasionally and brushing with orange
  mixture, about 10 minutes or until browned
  lightly. Serve with yogurt.

Soak bamboo skewers in water for at least
an hour before using, to avoid scorching and
splintering during cooking.

fresh pineapple with coconut

1 small pineapple
⅓ cup passionfruit pulp
2 tablespoons coconut-
    flavored liqueur
¼ cup flaked coconut, toasted

prep + cook time 10 minutes
serves 4

1 Peel and core pineapple; slice thinly.
2 Divide pineapple among serving dishes;
  drizzle with passionfruit and liqueur, sprinkle
  with coconut.

summer fruit in blackcurrant syrup

We used apricots, plums, nectarines and peaches. Cherries and berries can also be used.

 1 vanilla bean
1½ cups blackcurrant syrup
 2 pounds stone fruit, halved, stones removed
 6 ounces vanilla-flavored Greek yogurt

prep + cook time 30 minutes
serves 4

1 Split vanilla bean in half lengthways; scrape seeds into large saucepan. Add pod, syrup and ½ cup water to pan; bring to a boil. Boil, uncovered, about 5 minutes or until syrup thickens slightly. Add fruit, reduce heat; simmer, uncovered, turning fruit occasionally, about 8 minutes or until fruit is tender.
2 Remove fruit mixture from heat; discard vanilla bean. Serve fruit and syrup topped with yogurt.

poached pears with port

 1 large orange
 2 cups port
½ cup sugar
 8 pears, peeled

prep + cook time 1 hour
(plus cooling time)
serves 4

1 Cut 2 wide strips of zest from orange. Juice orange (you need 2 tablespoons).
2 Combine port, sugar, zest, juice and 6 cups water in large saucepan. Add pears; bring to a boil. Reduce heat; simmer, covered, about 20 minutes or until pears are tender. Cool pears in syrup.
3 Remove pears from syrup; strain syrup into medium heatproof bowl. Return 2 cups of the strained syrup to same pan (discard remaining syrup); bring to a boil. Boil, uncovered, about 15 minutes or until syrup is reduced to about ½ cup. Serve pears drizzled with syrup.

pears in cranberry syrup

3 cups cranberry juice

2/3 cup dry white wine

2 cardamom pods, bruised

4 bosc pears, peeled

prep + cook time 50 minutes
(+ cooling)
serves 4

1 Combine juice, wine and cardamom in large saucepan. Add pears; bring to the boil. Simmer, covered, about 25 minutes or until tender. Cool pears in syrup.

2 Remove pears from syrup; strain syrup into medium heatproof bowl. Return 2 cups of the strained syrup to same pan (discard remaining syrup); bring to a boil. Boil, uncovered, about 15 minutes or until syrup is reduced by half. Serve pears, hot or cold, with syrup.

tea-spiced pears

1 tablespoon jasmine tea leaves

1/3 cup firmly packed brown sugar

4 small pears

3 star anise

prep + cook time 35 minutes
serves 4

1 Combine tea leaves, sugar and 4 cups boiling water in large glass measuring cup; stir until sugar dissolves. Stand 10 minutes. Strain; discard leaves.

2 Meanwhile, peel, halve and core pears. Combine pears, strained tea mixture and star anise in medium saucepan; bring to a boil. Reduce heat, simmer, uncovered, about 25 minutes or until pears are tender. Transfer pears to bowls.

3 Boil syrup, uncovered, until reduced by half. Serve pears with syrup.

pears in cranberry syrup

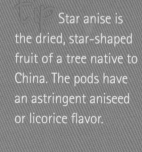

tip Pears can be made up to the end of step 1 a day ahead. Store pears in syrup, covered, in the fridge. Reheat pears and reduce the syrup just before serving.

tip Star anise is the dried, star-shaped fruit of a tree native to China. The pods have an astringent aniseed or licorice flavor.

tea-spiced pears

caramelized pears

4 pears
2 tablespoons butter
½ cup firmly packed brown
   sugar
2 tablespoons coffee-flavored
   liqueur

prep + cook time 25 minutes
serves 4

1 Peel and core pears; cut each pear into
   eight wedges.
2 Melt butter in large skillet, add pears; cook,
   stirring occasionally, until softened slightly.
3 Sprinkle sugar over pears; reduce heat. Cook,
   stirring occasionally, until sugar dissolves.
   Bring to a boil; boil 1 minute. Remove skillet
   from stove. Add liqueur; cook, over high heat,
   about 2 minutes or until mixture is syrupy.
4 Serve pears drizzled with syrup.

Serve with vanilla ice cream.

crêpes with ice cream and passionfruit sauce

¾ cup heavy cream
½ cup passionfruit pulp
1 package (12 ounces) frozen
   crêpes
4 cups vanilla ice cream

prep + cook time 10 minutes
serves 4

1 Warm cream in small saucepan over low heat;
   remove from heat, stir in passionfruit.
2 Heat crêpes according to package directions.
   Serve crêpes with sauce and ice cream.

tip Once you know how to make caramelized fruit, you'll be caramelizing everything from apples and pineapple to peaches and bananas. Serve them with vanilla ice cream.

caramelised pears

tip If passionfruit are not in season, the pulp in cans in the Latin foods section of the supermarket.

crêpes with ice cream and passionfruit sauce

broiled nectarines with yogurt

12 nectarines, halved and pitted
⅓ cup firmly packed light
    brown sugar
¼ cup orange juice
2 cups vanilla yogurt

prep + cook time 20 minutes
serves 6

1 Place nectarines, cut-side up, on baking sheet;
  sprinkle with brown sugar and juice. Place
  under preheated grill until browned lightly.
2 Serve nectarines with yogurt.

honey grilled figs

6 large figs
2 tablespoons sugar
¼ cup honey
1 teaspoon vanilla extract

prep + cook time 10 minutes
serves 6

1 Preheat broiler.
2 Cut figs in half lengthways. Place figs on
  baking sheet, cut-side up; sprinkle with sugar.
3 Broil about 5 minutes or until sugar melts
  and figs are lightly browned.
4 Meanwhile, combine honey and extract in
  small saucepan; stir over low heat, without
  boiling, until honey is runny.
5 Serve warm figs drizzled with honey mixture.

Serve with mascarpone cheese, if desired.

orange-caramelized apples

6 apples
4 tablespoons butter
¾ cup firmly packed light brown sugar
¼ cup orange-flavored liqueur

prep + cook time 25 minutes
serves 6

1 Peel and core apples; cut each apple into eight wedges.
2 Melt butter in large skillet, add apple; cook, stirring occasionally, until slightly softened.
3 Sprinkle sugar over apple; reduce heat. Cook, stirring occasionally, until sugar dissolves. Bring to a boil; boil 1 minute. Remove skillet from stove top. Add liqueur; cook, over high heat, about 2 minutes or until mixture is syrupy.
4 Serve apples drizzled with syrup.

Serve with heavy cream.

caramelized apples

4 tablespoons butter
½ cup firmly packed light brown sugar
4 apples, peeled, cored, quartered
8 scoops vanilla ice cream

prep + cook time 25 minutes
serves 8

1 Melt butter in small saucepan; stir in sugar and apples. Stir over low heat about 10 minutes or until sauce is thickened and apple is tender.
2 Serve apples with ice cream; drizzle over sauce.

Baked Desserts

There's nothing more comforting than the lingering smell of something sweet baked in the oven. And these simple recipes mean that no matter how short on time you are, you're only four ingredients away from a home-baked treat to enjoy at the end of the day.

34

scottish shortbread

1 cup (2 sticks) unsalted butter, chopped
½ cup sugar
¼ cup rice flour
2¼ cups all-purpose flour

prep + cook time
20 minutes
bake time 40 minutes
makes 16

1 Preheat oven to 300°F (275°F convection). Line two baking sheets with parchment paper.

2 Beat butter and ⅓ cup of the sugar in medium bowl with electric mixer until light and fluffy. Stir in sifted flours, in two batches. Knead on floured surface until smooth.

3 Divide mixture in half; shape into two 8-inch rounds on oven trays. Mark each round into eight wedges, prick with fork, pinch edges with fingers. Sprinkle with remaining sugar.

4 Bake about 40 minutes. Stand 5 minutes then, using sharp knife, cut into wedges along marked lines; cool on trays.

almond bread

3 egg whites
½ cup sugar
1 cup all-purpose flour
¾ cup almonds

prep + cook time 1 hour 35 minutes (+ cooling & standing)
makes 40

1 Preheat oven to 350°F (325°F convection). Coat a 4-inch x 8-inch loaf pan with cooking spray.

2 Beat egg whites in small bowl with electric mixer until soft peaks form. Gradually add sugar, beating until dissolved between additions.

3 Fold sifted flour and nuts into egg white mixture, spread mixture into pan; bake about 30 minutes. Cool bread in pan. Remove bread from pan, wrap in foil; stand overnight.

4 Preheat oven to 300°F (275°F convection).

5 Using a sharp serrated knife, cut the bread into wafer-thin slices. Place slices, in single layer, on ungreased oven trays. Bake about 45 minutes or until dry and crisp.

scottish shortbread

tip Don't overbake your shortbread. It should be a pale golden color, no darker. The stiff shortbread dough retains it shape well during baking, making it perfect for cutting into stars or other shapes for Christmas treats or other special occasions.

almond bread

tip Almond bread is an excellent accompaniment to desserts such as mousse, sorbet or ice-cream or simply served with coffee. It will keep for months if stored in a sealed airtight container.

lemon butter cookies

1 cup (2 sticks) butter, softened
1 cup confectioners' sugar
1 teaspoon fresh lemon zest
2½ cups all-purpose flour

prep + cook time 30 minutes
(+ refrigeration)
makes 50

1 Beat butter, sifted confectioners' sugar and zest in small bowl with electric mixer until light and fluffy. Transfer mixture to large bowl; stir in flour, in two batches.

2 Knead dough on lightly floured surface until smooth. Divide dough in half; roll each half into a 10-inch log. Wrap in plastic wrap; refrigerate about 1 hour or until firm.

3 Preheat oven to 350°F (325°F convection). Line two baking sheets with parchment paper.

4 Cut logs into ½-inch slices; place on sheets about ¾ inch apart.

5 Bake about 10 minutes or until lightly browned. Transfer cookies onto wire rack to cool.

honey butter cookies

8 tablespoons (1 stick) butter, softened
⅓ cup honey
¾ cup all-purpose flour
¼ cup cornstarch

prep + cook time 35 minutes
makes 24

1 Preheat oven to 350°F (325°F convection). Line two baking sheets with parchment paper.

2 Beat butter and honey in small bowl with electric mixer until light and fluffy; stir in flour and cornstarch. Spoon mixture into piping bag fitted with ½-inch fluted tip.

3 Pipe stars about 1 inch apart onto sheets. Bake about 15 minutes; cool cookies on sheets.

vanilla bean butter biscuits

8 tablespoons (1 stick) butter, softened
½ cup confectioners' sugar
1 vanilla bean
1¼ cups all-purpose flour

prep + cook time 30 minutes (+ refrigeration)
makes 22

1 Place butter and sifted confectioners' sugar in small bowl. Split vanilla bean; scrape seeds into bowl. Beat with electric mixer until light and fluffy; stir in sifted flour, in two batches.
2 Knead dough on floured surface until smooth. Shape dough into 9-inch rectangular log. Enclose log in plastic wrap; refrigerate about 30 minutes or until firm.
3 Preheat oven to 350°F (325°F convection). Line two baking sheets with parchment paper.
4 Cut log into ½-inch slices; place slices about ¾ inch apart on sheets. Bake about 12 minutes. Cool on sheets.

maple-syrup butter cookies

8 tablespoons (1 stick) butter, softened
⅓ cup maple syrup
¾ cup all-purpose flour
¼ cup finely ground cornmeal

prep + cook time 35 minutes
makes 24

1 Preheat oven to 350°F (325°F convection). Line 2 baking sheets with parchment paper.
2 Beat butter and maple syrup in small bowl with electric mixer until light and fluffy; stir in flour and cornmeal. Spoon mixture into piping bag fitted with ½-inch fluted tip.
3 Pipe stars about 1½ inches apart onto sheets. Bake about 15 minutes; cool cookies on baking sheets.

orange butter cookies

1 cup (2 sticks) unsalted butter, softened
1 cup confectioners' sugar
1 teaspoon fresh orange zest
2½ cups all-purpose flour

prep + cook time 30 minutes
(plus refrigeration time)
makes 50

1 Beat butter, sifted confectioners' sugar and zest in small bowl with electric mixer until light and fluffy. Transfer to large bowl.
2 Stir sifted flour, in two batches, into butter mixture. Knead dough on lightly floured surface until smooth. Divide dough in half; roll each half into a 10-inch log. Enclose in plastic wrap; refrigerate about 1 hour or until firm.
3 Preheat oven to 350°F (325°F convection).
4 Cut rolls into ½-inch slices; place 1 inch apart on baking sheets lined with parchment paper. Bake about 10 minutes or until browned lightly. Transfer cookies onto wire racks to cool.

amaretti

1 cup ground almonds
1 cup sugar
2 egg whites
¼ teaspoon almond extract

prep + cook time 30 minutes
(+ standing)
makes 20

1 Lightly coat two baking sheets with cooking spray.
2 Beat ground almonds, sugar, egg whites and extract in small bowl with electric mixer for 3 minutes; stand 5 minutes.
3 Spoon mixture into piping bag fitted with ½-inch plain tip. Pipe directly onto trays in circular motion from center out, to make cookies about 1½ inches in diameter. Cover unbaked cookies loosely with foil; stand at room temperature overnight.
4 Preheat oven to 350°F (275°F convection).
5 Bake cookies about 12 minutes. Leave on baking sheets 5 minutes; transfer to wire rack to cool.

chocolate butter cookies

1 cup (2 sticks) butter, softened
1 cup confectioners' sugar
2½ cups all-purpose flour
4 ounces dark chocolate, melted

prep + cook time 30 minutes
(+ refrigeration)
makes 50

1 Beat butter and sifted confectioners' sugar in small bowl with electric mixer until light and fluffy. Transfer to large bowl.
2 Stir sifted flour, in two batches, into butter mixture. Knead dough on lightly floured surface until smooth. Divide dough in half; roll each half into a 10-inch log. Enclose in plastic wrap; refrigerate about 1 hour or until firm.
3 Preheat oven to 350°F (325°F convection). Coat two baking sheets with cooking spray.
4 Cut rolls into ½-inch slices; place on sheets ¾ inch apart. Bake about 10 minutes or until lightly browned. Transfer cookies onto wire racks to cool.

almond and chocolate cookies

3 cups ground almonds
1 cup sugar
3 egg whites, lightly beaten
4 ounces milk chocolate, melted

prep + cook time 30 minutes
makes 24

1 Preheat oven to 350°F (325°F convection). Line two baking sheets with parchment paper.
2 Combine ground almonds, sugar and egg whites in large bowl with 2 tablespoons of water; stir until mixture forms a firm paste.
3 Roll level tablespoons of mixture into balls; place on trays 1 inch apart; flatten with hand. Bake about 15 minutes; cool cookies on trays. Drizzle with melted chocolate.

almond cookies

3 cups ground almonds
1 cup sugar
3 egg whites, lightly beaten
1 cup sliced almonds

prep + cook time 45 minutes
makes 25

1 Preheat oven to 350°F (325°F convection).
  Line two baking sheets with parchment paper.
2 Combine ground almonds and sugar in large
  bowl. Add egg whites; stir until mixture forms
  a firm paste. Place nuts in medium shallow
  tray. Roll level tablespoons of the mixture
  through nuts; roll into 3-inch logs. Shape logs
  to form crescents.
3 Place crescents on prepared trays; bake about
  15 minutes or until lightly browned.

coconut macaroons

1 egg, separated
1 egg yolk
¼ cup sugar
1²/₃ cups shredded coconut

prep + cook time 1 hour (+ cooling)
makes 18

1 Preheat oven to 300°F (275°F convection).
  Line two baking sheets with parchment paper.
2 Beat egg yolks and sugar in small bowl until
  creamy; stir in coconut.
3 Beat egg white in small bowl until firm peaks
  form; stir gently into coconut mixture.
4 Drop heaped teaspoons of the mixture onto
  baking sheets.
5 Bake 15 minutes. Reduce heat to 250°F (225°F
  convection); bake about 30 minutes or until
  golden brown; loosen macaroons, cool on trays.

almond biscuits

tip Store almond cookies in an airtight container for up to two weeks.

coconut macaroons

tip Store in an airtight container for up to three weeks. Macaroons are suitable to freeze for up to three months.

apricot chewies

3 egg whites

½ cup sugar

¾ cup coarsely chopped
    macadamias

¾ cup chopped dried apricots

prep + cook time 35 minutes

makes 18

1 Preheat oven to 325°F (300·F convection).
   Line two baking sheets with parchment paper.

2 Beat egg whites in small bowl with electric
   mixer until soft peaks form. Gradually add
   sugar, beating until sugar dissolves. Transfer
   to medium bowl; fold in nuts and apricots,
   in two batches.

3 Drop heaped tablespoons of mixture about
   1½ inches apart onto trays; bake about
   30 minutes. Let stand 5 minutes before
   transferring to wire rack to cool.

fruity macaroons

3 egg whites

¾ cup sugar

½ cup flaked coconut

½ cup finely chopped
    dried apricots

prep + cook time 30 minutes

makes 24

1 Preheat oven to 300°F (275°F convection).
   Line two baking sheets with parchment paper.

2 Beat egg whites in small bowl with electric
   mixer until soft peaks form. Gradually add
   sugar, beating until sugar dissolves. Transfer
   to large bowl; fold in coconut and apricots.

3 Drop heaped tablespoons of mixture about
   2 inches apart onto baking sheets; bake about
   20 minutes. Cool on sheets.

almond macaroons

2 egg whites
½ cup sugar
1¼ cups almond meal
2 tablespoons plain flour

prep + cook time 30 minutes
makes 22

1 Preheat oven to 300°F (275°F convection). Line two baking sheets with parchment paper..
2 Beat egg whites in small bowl with electric mixer until soft peaks form; gradually add sugar, beating until dissolved between additions. Gently fold in almond meal and sifted flour, in two batches.
3 Drop level tablespoons of mixture about 2 inches apart on baking sheets; bake about 20 minutes or until firm and dry. Cool on sheets.

brandy snaps

4 tablespoons butter
⅓ cup firmly packed brown sugar
2 tablespoons golden syrup
⅓ cup all-purpose flour

prep + cook time 30 minutes
makes 18

1 Preheat oven to 375°F (350°F convection). Line two baking sheets with parchment paper..
2 Combine butter, sugar and syrup in small saucepan; stir over low heat until smooth. Remove from heat; stir in sifted flour.
3 Drop rounded teaspoons of mixture about 2 inches apart on baking sheets. Bake about 7 minutes or until snaps bubble.
4 Slide spatula under each snap to loosen; working quickly, wrap one snap around handle of a wooden spoon. Remove handle; place snap on wire rack to cool. Repeat with the remaining snaps.
5 If you like, fill the snaps with whipped cream, before serving.

coffee hazelnut meringues

2 egg whites
½ cup sugar
2 teaspoons instant coffee
¼ cup roasted hazelnuts

prep + cook time 55 minutes
(plus cooling time)
makes 30

1 Preheat oven to 250°F (225°F convection).
  Line two baking sheets with parchment paper.
2 Beat egg whites in small bowl with electric
  mixer until soft peaks form. Gradually add
  sugar, beating until dissolved between
  additions.
3 Meanwhile, dissolve coffee in 2 teaspoons
  hot water in small bowl. Fold coffee mixture
  into meringue mixture.
4 Spoon mixture into piping bag fitted with
  2-inch fluted tip. Pipe meringues onto sheets
  1-inch apart; top each meringue with a nut.
5 Bake about 45 minutes. Cool meringues in
  oven with door ajar.

caramel meringue tarts

18 gingersnap cookies
1 jar (12 ounces) caramel
  filling
2 egg whites
⅓ cup sugar

prep + cook time 30 minutes
makes 18

1 Preheat oven to 325°F (300°F convection). Coat
  18 holes of two 12-hole (1½-tablespoons)
  shallow muffin pans with cooking spray.
2 Place one cookies over top of each greased pan
  hole; bake about 4 minutes or until cookies
  soften. Using the back of a teaspoon, gently
  push softened cookies into pan holes; cool.
3 Increase oven temperature to 475°F (450°F
  convection).
4 Place caramel in small bowl; whisk until smooth.
  Spoon caramel into cookies.
5 Beat egg whites in small bowl with electric
  mixer until soft peaks form; gradually add sugar,
  beating until sugar dissolves. Spread meringue
  over caramel; bake pies about 3 minutes or until
  meringue is lightly browned.

tip These versatile little bliss bombs are best served as a post-dessert accompaniment with freshly brewed coffee.

coffee hazelnut meringues

tip These little tarts look so impressive but are super simple to make—you'll fool everyone into thinking you've spent hours in the kitchen preparing them. For a little garnish, sprinkle some shredded coconut on top of the meringue toppings before you bake them.

caramel meringue tarts

apricot and honey soufflés

¼ cup sugar

4 apricots

2 tablespoons honey

4 egg whites

prep + cook time 45 minutes
serves 6

1 Preheat oven to 375°F (350°F convection). Coat six ¾-cup soufflé dishes with cooking spray; sprinkle inside of dishes with a little of the sugar, place on baking sheet.

2 Place apricots in small heatproof bowl, cover with boiling water; stand 2 minutes. Drain; cool 5 minutes then peel apricots and remove the pits. Chop apricot flesh finely.

3 Combine apricot in small saucepan with remaining sugar, honey and ¼ cup water; bring to a boil. Reduce heat; simmer, uncovered, about 10 minutes or until apricots soften to a jam-like consistency.

4 Beat egg whites in small bowl with electric mixer until soft peaks form. With motor operating, gradually add hot apricot mixture, beating until just combined.

5 Divide mixture among dishes; bake 15 minutes. Dust with sifted confectioners' sugar, if desired.

rhubarb soufflé

½ cup caster sugar

1½ cups chopped coarsely rhubarb

3 egg whites

1 tablespoon confectioners' sugar

prep + cook time 30 minutes
serves 4

1 Preheat oven to 400°F (375°F convection).

2 Grease four 1-cup ovenproof dishes; sprinkle base and sides with 2 tablespoons of the sugar. Stand dishes on baking sheet.

3 Combine rhubarb, 2 tablespoons of the sugar and 2 tablespoons water in small saucepan. Cook, stirring, over medium heat, about 10 minutes or until mixture thickens. Transfer mixture to medium heatproof bowl.

4 Meanwhile, beat egg whites in small bowl with electric mixer until soft peaks form. Gradually add remaining sugar; beat until firm peaks form.

5 Fold egg-white mixture into warm rhubarb mixture, in two batches. Spoon mixture into dishes. Bake in oven about 12 minutes.

6 Serve soufflés immediately, dusted with sifted confectioners' sugar.

tip Famous for their delicate texture, soufflés have a reputation for being temperamental to cook (or to keep risen), but they are relatively easy to create. The key is to eat them as soon as they emerge from the oven. They will start to deflate within minutes.

apricot and honey soufflés

tip Rhubarb has thick, celery-like stalks that are the only edible part of the plant—the leaves contain a toxic substance and should be discarded. Although eaten as a fruit, rhubarb is actually a vegetable.

rhubarb soufflé

mini fruit pies

2 discs unbaked pie dough
1 cup fruit filling
2 teaspoons sugar

prep + cook time 35 minutes
makes 12

1 Preheat oven to 400°F (375°F convection).
Coat a 12-hole (1-tablespoon) mini muffin
pan with cooking oil spray.
2 Cut 2¼-inch rounds from pie dough; press
into pan holes. Cut 1½-inch rounds from
remaining dough. Divide fruit filling among
pastry cases; top with rounds. Press edges
firmly to seal. Brush tops lightly with water;
sprinkle with sugar. Make small cut in pie tops.
3 Bake about 20 minutes. Stand pies in pan
10 minutes before turning, top-side up, onto
wire rack. Serve pies warm or cold.

berry and cream pastries

2 sheets frozen puff pastry,
thawed
2 tablespoons confectioners'
sugar
1½ pounds mixed fresh berries
2 cups heavy cream, whipped

prep + cook time 40 minutes
serves 8

1 Preheat oven to 425°F (400°F
convection). Line two baking
sheets with parchment paper.
2 Cut one pastry sheet in half.
Sprinkle one half with 2 teaspoons
of sifted confectioners' sugar;
place remaining pastry half on top.

Roll pastry up tightly from short side; cut log
into eight rounds. Repeat with remaining pastry
sheet and another 2 teaspoons of the sifted
confectioners' sugar.
3 Place rounds, cut-side up, on board dusted with
confectioners' sugar; roll each round into an
oval about 3 inches x 4 inches.
4 Place ovals on prepared trays. Bake about
12 minutes or until pastries are lightly browned
and crisp, turning halfway through baking.
5 Place a drop of whipped cream on each of eight
plates (to stop pastry sliding); top each with one
pastry. Divide half the berries over pastries, top
with whipped cream, remaining berries and
remaining pastries. Dust with remaining sifted
confectioners' sugar.

plum and hazelnut mini tarts

1 sheet frozen puff pastry, thawed

¼ cup demerara sugar

⅓ cup finely chopped hazelnuts

9 canned plums in natural juice, drained

prep + cook time 20 minutes
makes 9

1 Preheat oven to 350°F (325°F convection). Line two baking sheets with parchment paper.

2 Cut pastry into 9 squares; place on tray, prick pastry with fork.

3 Divide sugar and nuts among pastry squares, leaving ½-inch border around each.

4 Halve plums; discard. Divide among pastry squares. Bake about 10 minutes or until pastry is golden brown.

apricot and almond tarts

2 sheets frozen puff pastry, thawed

½ cup demerara sugar

⅔ cup finely chopped almonds

12 canned apricot halves in natural juice, drained

prep + cook time 20 minutes
serves 8

1 Preheat oven to 350°F (325°F convection). Coat two baking sheets with parchment paper.

2 Cut pastry into quarters; place quarters on sheets; prick with fork. Sprinkle over sugar and nuts, leaving ½-inch border.

3 Slice apricot halves thinly; divide among pastry squares. Bake about 10 minutes or until pastry is golden brown.

peach and walnut galettes

1 sheet frozen puff pastry, thawed

¼ cup sugar

⅓ cup finely chopped walnuts

4 canned peach halves in natural juice, drained

prep + cook time 20 minutes
makes 4

1 Preheat oven to 375°F (350°F convection). Line sheet with baking parchment paper.

2 Cut pastry into quarters; place quarters on tray, prick pastry with fork.

3 Divide sugar and nuts among pastry squares, leaving ½-inch border around each.

4 Slice peach halves thinly; divide among pastry squares. Bake about 10 minutes or until pastry is golden brown.

banana tarte tatin

1¼ cups sugar

8 tablespoons (1 stick) cold unsalted butter, chopped

1 sheet frozen puff pastry, thawed

4 large bananas, peeled, cut into ¾-inch pieces

prep + cook time 35 minutes
serves 4

1 Combine 1 cup of the sugar with 2 tablespoons water in medium saucepan; stir over heat, without boiling, until sugar is dissolved. Bring to a boil; boil, uncovered, without stirring, about 10 minutes or until a caramel color, remove from heat. Gradually whisk butter into caramel to form a sauce; pour into 8-inch ovenproof skillet. Cool.

2 Meanwhile, preheat oven to 425°F (400°F convection).

3 Cut 9-inch circle from pastry.

4 Place banana on top of caramel; top with pastry. Tuck in overhanging pastry; sprinkle with remaining sugar.

5 Bake 15 minutes or until pastry is browned and cooked through. Invert onto warmed plate to serve.

peach and walnut galettes

banana tarte tatin

tip Galette is the general French name for a freeform rustic tart, usually consisting of a thin layer of fruit baked on top of a buttery, crisp pastry base. Serve this galette warm, straight from the oven, with a good dollop of whipped cream.

tips Use a metal whisk to incorporate butter into caramel. Serving the tarte tartin on a warmed plate keeps the caramel soft. Serve with ice-cream or whipped cream, if desired.

roasted pear tart

1 sheet frozen puff pastry, thawed

1 jar (28 ounces) can pear halves in natural juice, drained

1 tablespoon pure maple syrup

1 tablespoon butter, melted

prep + cook time 30 minutes
serves 4

1 Preheat oven to 400°F (375°F convection). Line a baking sheet with parchment paper.

2 Cut pastry sheet in half; place pastry halves about 1 inch apart on prepared tray.

3 Place three pear halves, cut-side down, on each pastry half; brush pears with combined syrup and butter. Bake, uncovered, about 20 minutes or until pastry is puffed and browned lightly.

4 To serve, cut in half, and accompany with ice cream or whipped cream, if desired.

apple tarte tatin

8 tablespoons (1 stick) unsalted butter, coarsely chopped

6 large apples, peeled, cored, quartered

1 cup firmly packed light brown sugar

2 discs unbaked pie dough

prep + cook time 1 hour 45 minutes
serves 8

1 Melt butter in large heavy skillet; add apple, sprinkle with sugar. Cook, uncovered, over low heat, for about 1 hour, turning apples as they caramelize.

2 Preheat oven to 400°F (375°F convection).

3 Place apple, rounded-sides down, in 9-inch deep-dish pie plate; drizzle with 1 tablespoon of the caramel. Reserve remaining caramel.

4 Top apples with dough, cutting extra dough to fit pan. Tuck dough carefully around apple.

5 Bake tarte tatin about 30 minutes or until crust is browned. Carefully turn onto serving plate, apple-side up; drizzle apple with reheated reserved caramel.

roasted apple tart

2 sheets frozen puff pastry, thawed

2 cans (28 ounces) apple slices, drained

2 tablespoons pure maple syrup

4 tablespoons butter, melted

prep + cook time 30 minutes
serves 8

1 Preheat oven to 400°F (375°F convection). Coat two baking sheets with cooking spray.

2 Cut each pastry sheet in half; place pastry halves about 3/4 inch apart on trays.

3 Arrange apple slices over pastry; brush apple with combined syrup and butter. Bake about 20 minutes or until pastry is puffed and lightly browned.

raspberry croissant pudding

5 croissants, thinly sliced

1/3 cup raspberry jam

3 cups heavy cream

4 eggs

prep + cook time 1 hour 15 minutes
serves 8

1 Preheat oven to 325°F (300°F convection).

2 Coat shallow 8-cup ovenproof dish with cooking spray. Layer croissant slices, overlapping slightly, in dish; dollop spoonfuls of jam over slices.

3 Whisk cream and eggs in large bowl until combined; pour over croissants in dish.

4 Place dish in large baking dish; add enough boiling water to come halfway up sides of ovenproof dish. Bake about 1 hour or until pudding sets. Remove pudding from baking dish; stand 5 minutes before serving with some fresh raspberries and vanilla ice cream, if desired.

baked apples

4 large Granny Smith apples
3 tablespoons butter, melted
⅓ cup firmly packed brown
    sugar
½ cup raisins

prep + cook time 1 hour
serves 4

1 Preheat oven to 325°F (300°F convection).
2 Core unpeeled apples about three-quarters of the way down from stem end, making hole 2 inches in diameter. Use small sharp knife to score around center of each apple.
3 Combine remaining ingredients in small bowl. Pack raisin mixture firmly into apples; stand apples upright in small baking dish. Bake, uncovered, about 45 minutes.

mini toffee apples

2 red apples
1 tablespoon lemon juice
3 cups sugar

prep + cook time 1 hour (+ cooling)
makes 24

1 Preheat oven to 225°F (200°F convection). Coat two 12-hole (1-tablespoon) mini muffin pans with cooking spray.
2 Cut unpeeled apples into ¼-inch cubes; combine in small bowl with juice. Spread apple onto baking sheet lined with parchment paper. Bake about 40 minutes or until dried.
3 Meanwhile, stir sugar and 1 cup of water in medium heavy-based saucepan over heat until sugar dissolves. Bring to a boil; boil about 10 minutes, without stirring, or until toffee turns golden brown. Remove pan from heat; allow bubbles to subside.
4 Divide apple among pan holes. Pour toffee slowly over apple; cool about 10 minutes.
5 Cut each popsicle stick in half. Position half a stick, cut-side down, in center of each toffee; cool. Using sharp, pointed knife, carefully insert down one side of each pan hole to loosen toffee from edge of pan.

baked apples

tip Granny Smith apples have a bright green skin and are crisp, juicy and tart, which makes them versatile in cooking and perfect for baking in pies, stewing and for sauces and spreads.

tips Red delicious are the best apples to use. You need 12 popsicle sticks for this recipe. Gently twist the sticks then pull to remove toffees from pan. Using a saucepan with a pouring lip makes it easy to pour the toffee into the pans.

mini toffee apples

lemon meringue tarts

12 small frozen sweet tart shells
1 jar (11 ounces) lemon curd
3 egg whites
3/4 cup sugar

prep + cook time 25 minutes
makes 12

1 Preheat oven to 350°F (325°F convection).
2 Place tart shells on baking sheet; bake 10 minutes, cool. Increase oven temperature to 475°F (450°F convection).
3 Fill tart shells with lemon curd.
4 Beat egg whites in small bowl with electric mixer until soft peaks form; gradually add sugar, beating until sugar dissolves between additions. Pipe or spoon meringue over lemon curd.
5 Return tarts to oven; bake about 5 minutes or until meringue is lightly browned.

crème brûlée

1 vanilla bean, split in half lengthways
3 cups heavy cream
6 egg yolks
1/2 cup sugar

prep + cook time 55 minutes (+ refrigeration)
serves 6

1 Preheat oven to 350°F (325°F convection. Grease six 1/2-cup ovenproof dishes.
2 Scrape vanilla seeds into small saucepan; add pod and cream. Heat mixture without boiling.
3 Place egg yolks and half the sugar in medium bowl; whisk in hot cream mixture. Set bowl over medium saucepan of simmering water; stir about 10 minutes or until custard thickens and coats the back of a spoon; discard pod.
4 Place dishes in large baking dish; divide custard among dishes. Add enough boiling water to baking dish to come halfway up sides of ovenproof dishes. Bake about 20 minutes or until set. Remove from dish; cool. Cover; refrigerate overnight. Make brûlée topping according to the instructions in the tip at right.

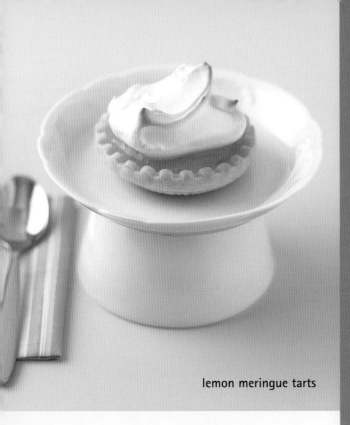

lemon meringue tarts

tip Lemon curd, also known as lemon butter, is available in jars from most supermarkets. Look for it in the baking section. You could use your favorite jam or caramel instead of the lemon curd.

crème brûlée

tips To make brûlée topping preheat broiler. Place custards in shallow flameproof dish filled with ice cubes; sprinkle custards evenly with remaining sugar. Using finger, spread sugar over the surface of each custard, pressing in gently; grill until the tops caramelize. You can also use a small blowtorch to caramelize the brûlée tops. Store leftover egg whites in the fridge or freeze them in an airtight container for later use. Try making a pavlova, or meringues.

Fridge & Freezer Desserts

Finish your meal on a high note with a sweet treat you pull from the fridge or freezer. Fresh and fruity, or decadent and sinful—there's something to suit any menu in this easy-to-assemble collection.

34

watermelon and berry salad

4 pounds seedless watermelon

½ pound strawberries, halved

¼ pound fresh blueberries

¼ cup loosely packed fresh
   mint

prep time 10 minutes

serves 4

1 Using melon baller, cut out watermelon balls.

2 Combine watermelon in medium bowl with berries and mint.

watermelon, raspberry and cranberry salad

1 pound watermelon, cut into
   1-inch pieces

1 cup fresh raspberries

½ cup cranberry juice

¼ cup fresh mint

prep time 10 minutes (+ refrigeration)

serves 2

1 Combine ingredients in medium bowl.
  Refrigerate 15 minutes.

tip This fruit salad is delicious and loaded with healthy goodness. Blueberries are full of antioxidants and have been shown to lower cholesterol. If you don't have a melon baller just cut the watermelon into even-sized square chunks.

watermelon and berry salad

tip This refreshing and bright ruby red fruit salad is excellent at any time of day, and is great served with a dollop of fruity yogurt on top.

watermelon, raspberry and cranberry salad

melon tiramisu

1 cup heavy cream
2 round sponge cakes
(7-inches)
¼ cup melon-flavored liqueur
1¼ pounds mixed melon,
chopped coarsely

prep time 25 minutes
serves 6

1 Beat cream in small bowl with electric mixer
until soft peaks form.
2 Split cakes in half horizontally; trim brown
edges. Cut 12 rounds from cakes (3 inches
each). Place one cake round in each of six
1½ cup glasses; drizzle with half the liqueur.
3 Divide half the combined melons then cream
over cake. Repeat layering.

strawberries romanoff

1 pound strawberries, halved
1½ tablespoons orange-flavored
liqueur
¼ cup confectioners' sugar
½ cup heavy cream

prep + cook time
10 minutes (plus refrigeration time)
serves 4

1 Combine strawberries, liqueur and 2 tablespoons
of the sifted confectioners' sugar in large bowl;
refrigerate 30 minutes. Drain strawberries over
small bowl; reserve liquid. Divide three-quarters
of the strawberries among serving dishes.
2 Blend or process remaining strawberries,
remaining sifted confectioners' sugar and
reserved liquid until smooth. Beat cream in
small bowl with electric mixer until soft peaks
form; fold in strawberry mixture.
3 Top strawberries with strawberry cream.

melon tiramisu

tip We used Midori in this recipe, a honeydew melon-flavored liqueur. Cantaloupe is also known as musk melon; it is related to the honeydew and watermelon.

strawberries romanoff

tip We used Grand Marnier orange-flavored liqueur but you can use orange juice if you don't want the alcohol.

raspberry almond creams

1 cups heavy cream
2/3 cup thick vanilla custard
4 ounces almond macaroons, crumbled
1 cup raspberries

prep + cook time 15 minutes
serves 6

1 Whip cream in small bowl with electric mixer until soft peaks form; transfer to medium bowl.
2 Fold in custard and crumbled macaroon. Layer into serving glasses with raspberries.

berry mousse

2 teaspoons gelatin
2 egg whites
1/3 cup sugar
2 cartons (6 ounces each) berry-flavored yogurt

prep + cook time 10 minutes
(plus refrigeration time)
serves 4

1 Sprinkle gelatin over 2 tablespoons water in small heatproof bowl; place bowl in small pan of simmering water, stir until gelatin dissolves, cool.
2 Beat egg whites in small bowl with electric mixer until soft peaks form. Gradually add sugar, beating until sugar dissolves.
3 Place yogurt in medium bowl; stir in gelatin mixture, fold in egg white mixture. Spoon mousse mixture into serving bowl, cover; refrigerate about 2 hours or until set. Serve mousse topped with mixed berries, if desired.

frozen passionfruit yogurt

½ cup sugar
1 teaspoon gelatin
2 cups plain yogurt
½ cup passionfruit pulp

prep + cook time 15 minutes
(+ freezing)
serves 4

1 Stir sugar and ¼ cup of water in small saucepan over low heat until sugar dissolves; transfer to medium bowl.
2 Sprinkle gelatin over sugar syrup, stirring until gelatin dissolves.
3 Combine yogurt and pulp with syrup. Pour yogurt mixture into loaf pan, cover tightly with foil; freeze 3 hours or until almost set.
4 Scrape yogurt mixture from bottom and sides of pan with fork; return to freezer until firm.

You need approximately six passionfruit for this recipe. Substitute with a ½ cup mashed peaches or berries, if desired.

yogurt and mixed berry pops

2 tablespoons water
1 teaspoon powdered gelatin
1½ cups frozen mixed berries, thawed
2 cups vanilla yogurt

prep + cook time 20 minutes
(+ freezing)
makes 8

1 Place the water in small heatproof bowl; sprinkle gelatin over water. Stand bowl in small saucepan of simmering water; stir until gelatin dissolves.
2 Blend or process berries until smooth; strain through fine sieve into large bowl, discard seeds.
3 Add yogurt and gelatin mixture to berry puree. Divide mixture evenly between eight (⅓-cup) popsicle moulds. Freeze 3 hours or overnight.

passionfruit sorbet

You need 12 medium passionfruit for this recipe.

1 cup passionfruit pulp
1 cup sugar
¼ cup lemon juice
2 egg whites

prep + cook time 30 minutes
(plus cooling and freezing time)
serves 8

1 Strain pulp into small bowl. Reserve seeds and juice separately.
2 Stir sugar and 2½ cups water in medium saucepan over high heat until sugar dissolves; bring to a boil. Reduce heat; simmer, uncovered, without stirring, 5 minutes. Transfer syrup to large heatproof bowl, cool to room temperature; stir in lemon juice and passionfruit juice.
3 Pour sorbet mixture into loaf pan, cover tightly with foil; freeze 3 hours or overnight.
4 Process mixture with egg whites until smooth; stir in reserved seeds. Return to loaf pan, cover; freeze until firm.

raspberry sorbet

¾ pound raspberries
1 cup sugar
1 tablespoon lemon juice
1 egg white

prep + cook time 30 minutes
(plus cooling and freezing time)
serves 8

1 Press raspberries through sieve into small bowl; discard seeds.
2 Stir sugar and 2½ cups water in medium saucepan over high heat until sugar dissolves; bring to a boil. Reduce heat; simmer, uncovered, without stirring, 5 minutes. Transfer syrup to large heatproof bowl, cool to room temperature; stir in raspberry pulp and lemon juice.
3 Pour sorbet mixture into loaf pan, cover tightly with foil; freeze 3 hours or overnight.
4 Process mixture with egg white until smooth. Return to loaf pan, cover; freeze until firm.

back left: lemon lime sorbet; back right: raspberry sorbet; front: passionfruit sorbet

lemon lime sorbet

2 limes
3 lemons
1 cup sugar
1 egg white

prep + cook time 30 minutes
(plus cooling and freezing time)
serves 8

1 Grate zest from limes (you need 1 tablespoon); juice limes (you need ¼ cup). Grate zest from lemons (you need 2 tablespoons); juice lemons (you need ½ cup).

2 Stir zests, sugar and 2½ cups water in medium saucepan over high heat until sugar dissolves; bring to a boil. Reduce heat; simmer, uncovered, without stirring, 5 minutes. Transfer syrup to large heatproof bowl, cool to room temperature; stir in juices.

3 Pour sorbet mixture into loaf pan, cover tightly with foil; freeze 3 hours or overnight.

4 Process mixture with egg white until smooth. Return to loaf pan, cover; freeze until firm.

turkish delight sundae

1 cup raspberries

4 cups vanilla ice cream

1 (2 ounces) chocolate-coated Turkish Delight bar, coarsely chopped

½ cup unsalted pistachios, roasted, coarsely chopped

prep time 10 minutes
serves 6

1 Blend or process raspberries until smooth.
2 Layer vanilla ice cream, raspberry puree, turkish delight and pistachios in serving glasses.

Use either fresh or thawed frozen raspberries for the sundae.

caramel banana split

1 cup caramel sauce

1½ cups heavy cream

8 small bananas

⅓ cup crushed peanuts

prep + cook time 15 minutes
serves 8

1 Whisk caramel and ¼ cup of the cream in small saucepan over low heat until smooth.
2 Beat remaining cream in small bowl with electric mixer until soft peaks form.
3 Peel then cut bananas lengthways; place in serving dishes. Top bananas with whipped cream; drizzle with sauce and sprinkle with nuts.

Serve with vanilla ice-cream if desired.

turkish delight sundae

tip Turkish delight is an extremely popular Middle-Eastern sweet that's available online and in Middle-Eastern groceries. Its Turkish name is rahat lokum— meaning 'rest for the throat'. It is a soft, jelly-like confection flavored with rosewater, which gives it its characteristic pale pink color.

caramel banana split

tip Caramel sauce can be made a day ahead; store in a screw-top jar or airtight container, in the fridge. Reheat sauce just before serving.

banana strawberry sundae

- 2 cups heavy cream
- 4 ounces mini meringues, coarsely chopped
- 4 bananas, sliced
- 2 pounds strawberries, coarsely chopped

1 Beat cream in small bowl with electric mixer until soft peaks form.
2 Layer cream, meringue, banana and strawberries among serving glasses.

prep time 15 minutes
serves 8

passionfruit and banana sundae

- 2 cups heavy cream
- 4 ounces vanilla meringue cookies, coarsely chopped
- 1 cup passionfruit pulp
- 8 small bananas, coarsely chopped

1 Beat cream in small bowl with electric mixer until soft peaks form.
2 Layer cream, meringue, passionfruit and banana among serving glasses.

prep time 15 minutes
serves 8

pineapple with coconut ice cream

½ pineapple, cut into 12 slices
¼ cup coconut-flavored liqueur
2 cups vanilla ice cream, slightly softened
½ cup shredded coconut, toasted

prep + cook time 10 minutes
serves 4

1 Brush pineapple with 1 tablespoon of the liqueur. Cook pineapple, in batches, in heated oiled large skillet until caramelized and heated through.
2 Meanwhile, combine ice cream, coconut and remaining liqueur in medium bowl.
3 Serve pineapple topped with scoops of coconut ice cream.

vanilla yogurt mousse

2 tablespoons gelatin
8 egg whites
1⅓ cups sugar
1 large container (32 ounces) yogurt

prep + cook time 10 minutes
(+ refrigeration)
serves 8

1 Sprinkle gelatin over ⅔ cup of water in medium heatproof bowl; place bowl in small pan of simmering water, stir until gelatin dissolves, cool.
2 Beat egg whites in large bowl with electric mixer until soft peaks form. Gradually add sugar, beating until sugar dissolves.
3 Place yogurt in medium bowl; stir in gelatin mixture, fold in egg white mixture. Spoon mousse mixture into serving bowl, cover; refrigerate about 2 hours or until set.

coffee hazelnut shots

⅓ cup hazelnut-flavored
   liqueur

2 tablespoons instant coffee

2 cups hazelnut gelato

¼ cup coarsely chopped
   hazelnuts

prep + cook time 20 minutes
serves 4

1 Combine liqueur, coffee and ¼ cup water in small saucepan; bring to a boil. Boil 2 minutes.

2 Divide gelato among four serving glasses; pour over coffee mixture. Serve sprinkled with hazelnuts.

chocolate mousse

6 ounces dark chocolate,
   coarsely chopped

2 tablespoons unsalted butter

3 eggs, separated

1¼ cups heavy cream, whipped

prep + cook time 25 minutes
(plus cooling and refrigeration time)
serves 6

1 Melt chocolate in medium heatproof bowl over medium saucepan of simmering water (don't let the water touch the base of the bowl). Remove from heat; add butter, stir until smooth. Stir in egg yolks. Transfer mixture to large bowl, cover; cool.

2 Beat egg whites in small bowl with electric mixer until soft peaks form. Fold egg whites and cream into chocolate mixture, in two batches.

3 Divide mousse among serving dishes; refrigerate 3 hours or overnight. Serve with extra whipped cream, chocolate curls and fresh raspberries, if desired.

coffee hazelnut shots

tip This smooth, sweet gelato is offset by the rich bitter coffee and punchy hazelnut liqueur, giving it a good kick.

chocolate mousse

tip The beauty of chocolate mousse, apart from the sheer pleasure of the taste, is that it can be made a day ahead. Make sure you fold (don't just stir) the egg whites and whipped cream with the chocolate to ensure the mousse is fluffy and light.

rhubarb crumble ice cream

2 cups coarsely chopped
rhubarb

2 tablespoons brown sugar

8 cups vanilla ice cream,
slightly softened

4 ounces gingersnap cookies,
coarsely chopped

prep + cook time 20 minutes
(plus freezing time)
serves 8

1 Line 5 x 9 inch loaf pan with plastic wrap.
2 Cook rhubarb and sugar in large heavy-based
saucepan, covered, about 5 minutes or until
rhubarb is almost tender. Reduce heat;
simmer, uncovered, about 5 minutes or until
rhubarb softens but retains its shape. Cool.
3 Place ice cream in large bowl; break up slightly.
Gently swirl in cookies and rhubarb mixture.
4 Pour ice cream mixture into prepared pan.
Cover; freeze 3 hours or until firm.

frozen green apple yogurt

*You need a green apple weighing just
over ½ pound for this recipe.*

⅓ cup honey

½ cup apple juice

¾ cup finely grated unpeeled
green apple

16 ounces Greek-style yogurt

prep + cook time 20 minutes
(plus freezing time)
serves 4

1 Stir honey and juice in small saucepan over low
heat until honey melts; cool syrup 5 minutes.
2 Combine honey mixture, apple and yogurt
in 5 x 9 inch loaf pan. Cover with foil; freeze
3 hours or overnight. Remove yogurt from
freezer 15 minutes before serving.

pink grapefruit granita

1 cup white sugar
1 cup fresh pink grapefruit
juice
¼ cup lemon juice
2 egg whites

prep + cook time 25 minutes
(plus freezing time)
serves 8

1 Stir the sugar and 1 cup water in small
saucepan over heat, without boiling, until
sugar dissolves. Bring to a boil; boil 5 minutes
without stirring. Remove from heat; stir in
juices, cool.
2 Beat egg whites in small bowl with electric
mixer until soft peaks form. Fold syrup into egg
white mixture; pour into 5 x 9 inch loaf pan.
Cover; freeze 3 hours or overnight.
3 Blend or process granita until pale and creamy.
Return to loaf pan, cover; freeze granita 3
hours or overnight.

watermelon and mint granita

1 cup sugar
3 pounds coarsely chopped
watermelon
2 cups firmly packed fresh
mint

prep + cook time 20 minutes
(plus freezing time)
serves 8

1 Combine sugar and 2 cups water
in medium saucepan. Stir over low
heat, without boiling, until sugar
dissolves; bring to a boil. Reduce
heat; simmer, uncovered, without

stirring, about 5 minutes or until syrup thickens
slightly but does not color.
2 Blend or process watermelon and mint, in
batches, until almost smooth; push batches
through sieve into large bowl. Add syrup; stir
to combine.
3 Pour mixture into two 9 x 13 baking dishes,
cover with foil; freeze about 3 hours or until
almost set.
4 Using fork, scrape granita from bottom and sides
of pans, mixing frozen with unfrozen mixture.
Cover, return to freezer. Repeat process every
hour for about 4 hours or until large ice crystals
form and granita has a dry, shard-like appearance.
Scrape again with fork before serving.

crunchy chocolate ice cream

7 ounces peanut brittle

18 small scoops dark chocolate
ice cream

4 ounces good-quality dark
chocolate, shaved

prep time 10 minutes
(plus refrigeration)
serves 6

1 Refrigerate brittle until ready to serve. Put
brittle into a strong plastic bag and coarsely
crush with a meat mallet or hammer.

2 Divide ice cream among 6 serving bowls.
Sprinkle over crushed brittle; top with
chocolate.

chocolate rocky road ice cream

4 cups chocolate ice cream

4½ ounces finely chopped
rocky road

3 ounces coarsely chopped
dark chocolate

½ cup heavy cream

prep + cook time 15 minutes
serves 4

1 Place ice cream in microwave-safe bowl.
Microwave on MEDIUM (50%) for 30 seconds
or until just softened. Stir in 3 ounces of the
rocky road. Freeze 10 minutes.

2 Meanwhile, stir chocolate and cream in small
saucepan over low heat until smooth.

3 Serve scoops of rocky road ice cream drizzled
with warm chocolate sauce. Sprinkle with
remaining rocky road.

crunchy chocolate ice cream

tip It's all about the chocolate, so choose the richest ice cream you can find and a chocolate high in cocoa solids.

chocolate rocky road ice cream

tip You can replace the rocky road with turkish delight, nuts or your favorite chocolate candy.

choc-cherry biscotti trifle

½ pound frozen pitted dark cherries, thawed

⅓ cup marsala

6 ounces chocolate hazelnut biscotti

12 ounces chocolate mousse

prep time 15 minutes

serves 4

1 Combine cherries and marsala in small bowl.
2 Reserve 8 biscotti; coarsely chop the remaining biscotti.
3 Place chocolate mousse in medium bowl; whisk until smooth.
4 Spoon half the cherry mixture into four 2-cup serving glasses; top with half the chopped biscotti and half the mousse. Repeat layering.
5 Serve trifles with reserved biscotti.

choc-peanut bombes

2 cups heavy cream

6 ounces dark chocolate, melted

½ cup coarsely chopped unsalted peanuts

3 Snickers bars, finely chopped

prep time 5 minutes
(+ refrigeration)

serves 8

1 Beat cream in small bowl with electric mixer until soft peaks form; add cooled chocolate, beat until combined. Fold in remaining ingredients; refrigerate 2 hours.

tip If you don't have marsala use hazelnut-flavoured liqueur or sweet sherry.

choc–cherry biscotti trifle

tip This recipe isn't suitable to freeze, but it divides easily if you want to prepare a smaller quantity (and you can enjoy ½ of a Snickers bar)!

choc–peanut bombes

plum and amaretti trifle

1 jar (28 ounces) canned whole
   plums, drained
1¼ cups heavy cream
¼ cup confectioners' sugar
4 ounces amaretti cookies,
   coarsely chopped

prep + cook time 15 minutes
serves 6

1 Halve plums, remove pits; cut each half into
  4 wedges.
2 Beat cream and sifted confectioners sugar in
  small bowl with electric mixer until soft peaks
  form. Crush cookies coarsely.
3 Divide half the plums among serving glasses;
  spoon half the cream mixture then half the
  crushed cookies over plums. Repeat with
  remaining plum halves, cream and cookies.

Serve sprinkled with sifted icing sugar, if desired.

crêpes with chocolate sauce

1½ cups heavy cream
6 ounces dark semi-sweet
   chocolate, coarsely chopped
1½ pounds frozen crêpes
6 cups vanilla ice cream

prep + cook time 10 minutes
serves 8

1 Bring cream to a boil in small saucepan; remove
  from heat. Add chocolate; stand 5 minutes. Stir
  until smooth.
2 Heat crêpes according to package directions.
  Serve crêpes with chocolate sauce and ice cream.

cranberry and port truffles

1 pound dark chocolate
¼ cup heavy cream
2 tablespoons port
⅓ cup dried cranberries, coarsely chopped

prep + cook time 45 minutes
(+ refrigeration & freezing)
makes 30

1 Coarsely chop 6½ ounces of the chocolate; melt remaining chocolate in heatproof bowl over saucepan of simmering water.
2 Combine cream and chopped chocolate in small saucepan; stir over low heat until smooth, stir in port and cranberries. Transfer to small bowl, cover; refrigerate 3 hours or overnight.
3 Working with a quarter of the chocolate mixture at a time (keeping remainder under refrigeration), roll rounded teaspoons into balls; place on tray. Freeze truffles until firm.
4 Working quickly, dip truffles in melted chocolate then roll gently in hands to coat evenly, return to tray; refrigerate until firm.

peanut butter and milk chocolate truffles

⅓ cup heavy cream
6 ounces milk chocolate, coarsely chopped
¼ cup unsalted crunchy peanut butter
¾ cup crushed peanuts

prep + cook time
45 minutes (plus refrigeration time)
makes 30

1 Combine cream and chocolate in small saucepan; stir over low heat until smooth, stir in peanut butter. Transfer to small bowl, cover; refrigerate 3 hours or overnight.
2 Working with a quarter of the chocolate mixture at a time (keeping remainder under refrigeration), roll rounded teaspoons into balls; place on tray. Refrigerate truffles until firm.
3 Working quickly, roll truffles in peanuts, return to tray; refrigerate truffles until firm.

dark chocolate and ginger truffles

⅓ cup heavy cream
6 ounces dark chocolate, coarsely chopped
½ cup candied ginger, finely chopped
¼ cup cocoa powder

prep + cook time
45 minutes (plus refrigeration time)
makes 30

1 Combine cream and chocolate in small saucepan; stir over low heat until smooth, stir in ginger. Transfer to small bowl, cover; refrigerate 3 hours or overnight.
2 Working with a quarter of the chocolate mixture at a time (keeping remainder under refrigeration), roll rounded teaspoons into balls; place on tray. Refrigerate truffles until firm.
3 Working quickly, roll truffles in sifted cocoa, return to tray; refrigerate truffles until firm.

white choc, lime and coconut truffles

½ cup coconut cream
2 teaspoons fresh lime zest
12 ounces white chocolate, coarsely chopped
1¼ cups shredded coconut

prep + cook time
45 minutes (plus refrigeration time)
makes 30

1 Combine coconut cream, zest and chocolate in small saucepan; stir over low heat until smooth. Transfer mixture to small bowl, cover; refrigerate 3 hours or overnight.
2 Working with a quarter of the chocolate mixture at a time (keeping remainder under refrigeration), roll rounded teaspoons into balls; place on tray. Refrigerate truffles until firm.
3 Working quickly, roll truffles in coconut, return to tray; refrigerate truffles until firm.

dark chocolate and ginger truffles

tip Chocolate truffles are a luxurious delicacy and best of all they're not hard to make. Be sure to use quality ingredients (chocolate makers around the world reserve their best ingredients for their truffles) and you'll have an impressive after-dinner finale everyone will love.

tip Hand-made treats make beautiful gifts. Boxed with pretty papers these delectable little artworks are a perfect idea for a special Christmas or birthday present.

white choc, lime and coconut truffles

frozen chocolate brownie pops

2 cups vanilla ice cream, softened

½ pound brownies, finely chopped

6 ounces semi-sweet chocolate chips

prep + cook time 20 minutes
(+ freezing)
makes 28

1 Grease two ice-cube trays. Line small baking sheets with parchment paper. Place 28 mini muffin paper cases on another small baking sheet.

2 Working quickly, combine ice-cream and brownies in medium bowl; press into ice-cube trays. Freeze about 2 hours until firm. Unmold onto tray; freeze a further 30 minutes.

3 Meanwhile, melt chocolate in medium heatproof bowl above medium saucepan of simmering water. Remove from heat; stand 5 minutes.

4 Using small cocktail toothpicks, dip ice cream blocks one at a time into chocolate to cover; place in paper case. Freeze until ready to serve.

chocolate fudge

¾ cup canned sweetened condensed milk

8 ounces dark semi-sweet chocolate chips, melted

1½ cups coarsely chopped toasted pecans

prep time 15 minutes
(+ refrigeration)
makes 18

1 Coat a 3¼-inch x 10-inch bar cake pan with cooking spray; line base and sides with parchment paper, extending paper 2 inches above long sides.

2 Combine ingredients in medium bowl. Spread mixture into pan.

3 Refrigerate several hours or overnight until firm.

frozen chocolate brownie pops

chocolate fudge

tip These little morsels improve with time. Make 1 or 2 days ahead to allow the flavors to intensify. Use rounded ice-cube trays if possible as the ice cream blocks will be easier to unmold. Pass a small knife around each block to help unmold. You could make this into a log. Press ice-cream mixture into bar pan lined with baking paper. Once frozen, place on wire rack and drizzle with melted chocolate to cover. Freeze until ready to serve, then cut into slices.

tip Any nut or combination of nuts can be used. Slice can be stored, wrapped in plastic wrap and refrigerated, for up to four weeks.

chocolate hazelnut tree

1 pound semi-sweet chocolate, melted
2 cups finely chopped toasted hazelnuts
1 brazil nut
2 teaspoons confectioners' sugar

prep time 30 minutes
(+ refrigeration)
makes 1

1 Line four baking sheets with parchment paper. Mark nine crosses, measuring 3 inches, 3½ inches, 4¼ inches, 5 inches, 5½ inches, 6 inches, 6¼ inches, 6¾ inches and 7 inches on trays, leaving about 1 inch space between each cross.
2 Combine the chocolate and hazelnuts in medium bowl. Drop teaspoonfuls of the chocolate mixture along all marked crosses to make branches; refrigerate several hours.
3 Assemble tree using instructions in the tip at right, refrigerate until chocolate sets between branches; dust with sifted icing sugar.

chocolate-dipped fruit

2½ cups milk chocolate melts
2 bananas, thickly sliced
½ pound strawberries
¾ cup dried apricots

prep + cook time 20 minutes
(+ refrigeration)
serves 4

1 Coat baking sheet with parchment paper.
2 Place chips in microwave-safe bowl; cook on MEDIUM-LOW (30%) in microwave oven for 1 minute. Using oven mitts, remove bowl from microwave oven; stir chocolate, return bowl to microwave oven. Repeat cooking and stirring two more times, for 1 minute the second time and about 1 minute the third time or until chocolate is melted.
3 Dip fruit, one piece at a time, into chocolate to coat about three-quarters of each piece of fruit. Place fruit in single layer on the prepared tray; refrigerate until set.

tip Drop about a teaspoon of the remaining melted chocolate into the center of a cake board; position the 7-inch branch on top. Assemble the remaining branches in pairs, starting from the largest branch and finishing with the smallest, using about a teaspoon of melted chocolate in the centre of each pair; refrigerate until set. Secure each pair to the next with chocolate. Secure brazil nut to the top with chocolate; drizzle with chocolate to cover it completely.

chocolate hazelnut tree

tip Use whatever fresh fruit is in season or any combination of dried fruit you like. Use dark or white chocolate if you prefer. Chocolate-dipped fruit is best eaten the day it is made.

chocolate-dipped fruit

34

Drinks

Whether you're looking for a detoxifying vegetable juice or a champagne cocktail, these recipes will inspire you to try a refreshing twist on your drink of choice.

lime and lemon grass spritzer

⅓ cup brown sugar

2 tablespoons coarsely
   chopped fresh lemon grass

½ cup lime juice

3 cups chilled sparkling
   mineral water

prep + cook time 15 minutes
(plus refrigeration time)
makes 4 cups

1 Place sugar and ½ cup water in small saucepan; stir over low heat until sugar dissolves. Remove from heat; stir in lemon grass. Cover; refrigerate until chilled.

2 Combine strained sugar mixture with lime juice, mineral water and 1 cup ice cubes in large jug.

raspberry cranberry crush

2 cups cranberry juice

2 tablespoons lemon juice

1 cup wildberry sorbet

1 cup frozen raspberries

prep time 5 minutes
makes 4 cups

1 Blend or process ingredients until smooth.

This tangy, bubbly lime and lemon grass combination is a refreshing drink for outdoor summer entertaining, and a great non-alcoholic offering to have on the table during the meal.

lime and lemon grass spritzer

This delicious, mega-healthy drink combines two super fruits—cranberries and raspberries—and there couldn't be a more pleasurable way to take in a dose of vitamin C, dietary fiber and antioxidants. And you will also be cleansing and purifying your system.

raspberry cranberry crush

homemade lemonade

4 lemons
4 cups sugar
5 quarts (20 cups) sparkling
  mineral water

prep + cook time 25 minutes
(plus cooling and refrigeration)
makes 25 cups

1 Remove zest from lemons using a vegetable
  peeler, avoiding white pith; reserve lemons.
2 Stir zest, sugar and 2 cups of water in large
  saucepan over low heat, without boiling,
  until sugar dissolves; bring to a boil. Simmer,
  uncovered, without stirring, about 10 minutes
  or until syrup is slightly thickened; cool.
3 Squeeze juice from lemons (you need 1 cup
  juice). Stir juice into syrup, strain into pitcher.
  Cover; keep refrigerated.
4 Just before serving, add four parts mineral
  water to one part lemonade, or to taste.

watermelon refresher

2 pounds coarsely chopped
  seedless watermelon
½ cup chilled orange juice
3 tablespoons lime juice

prep time 10 minutes
makes 4 cups

1 Blend or process ingredients until smooth.
  Garnish with lime slices, if desired.

melonade

½ cup lemon juice

2 tablespoons sugar

3 cups coarsely chopped watermelon

1½ cups chilled sparkling mineral water

prep + cook time 10 minutes
(plus cooling time)
makes 4 cups

1 Combine juice and sugar in small saucepan; stir over low heat until sugar dissolves. Cool.

2 Blend or process watermelon, in batches, until smooth; strain through sieve into large jug. Stir in lemon syrup and mineral water; serve immediately.

kiwi and mint frappé

4 medium kiwifruit, peeled, coarsely chopped

¼ cup apple juice

¼ cup coarsely chopped fresh mint

1 teaspoon sugar

prep time 5 minutes
serves 1

1 Blend or process ingredients with ¾ cup ice cubes until smooth.

2 Pour into glass; top with shredded mint, if desired.

apple and grapefruit juice

4 cups apple juice
4 cinnamon sticks, halved
lengthways
4 cups grapefruit juice

prep + cook time 10 minutes
(plus refrigeration)
makes 8 cups

1 Combine apple juice and cinnamon in medium saucepan; bring to a boil. Remove from heat; cool to room temperature. Transfer to large pitcher, cover; refrigerate 3 hours or overnight.
2 Add grapefruit juice to apple juice mixture; stir to combine.
3 Serve juice with cinnamon stick.

pineapple-orange frappé

1 pineapple, coarsely chopped
½ cup orange juice
3 cups crushed ice
1 tablespoon fresh orange zest

prep time 10 minutes
makes 4 cups

1 Blend or process pineapple and juice, in batches, until smooth.
2 Pour into large jug with crushed ice and zest; stir to combine.

apple and grapefruit juice

pineapple-orange frappé

tip You can use fresh or bottled grapefruit juice in this recipe. Ruby red grapefruit juice gives this drink a beautiful blush color. You will need to juice about 8 medium grapefruit for this recipe.

tip A frappé is best made just before serving as its thick, creamy texture will subside and separate if it stands for too long.

peach and raspberry juice

1 large peach, peeled, pitted,
   coarsely chopped
¼ cup fresh or frozen
   raspberries

1 Process ingredients until smooth; pour
   into glass.
2 Stir in ½ cup water; serve over ice.

prep time 5 minutes
serves 1

apple, pear and ginger juice

1 unpeeled apple, cored, cut
   into wedges
1 unpeeled pear, cored, cut
   into wedges
½-inch piece fresh ginger

1 Push ingredients through juice extractor into
   glass. Serve with ice.

prep time 5 minutes
serves 1

carrot, orange and ginger juice

1 large orange, peeled,
  quartered
1 medium carrot, coarsely
  chopped
½-inch piece fresh ginger

prep time 5 minutes
serves 1

1 Push ingredients through juice extractor into
glass. Serve with ice.

pomegranate and orange juice

⅔ cup pomegranate pulp
2 oranges, peeled, quartered

prep time 5 minutes
serves 1

1 Push ingredients through juice extractor into
glass; stir to combine.

sugar syrup

1 cup white sugar
1 cup water

prep + cook time 10 minutes
(+ cooling)
makes 1⅓ cups

1 Combine sugar and water in small saucepan; stir over low heat until sugar dissolves.
2 Bring to a boil, then reduce heat and simmer, uncovered, without stirring, 5 minutes; remove from heat, cool.

vanilla martini

1½ ounces vanilla-infused vodka
2 teaspoons sugar syrup
1 tablespoon frangelico
1 cup ice cubes

prep time 5 minutes
serves 1

1 Combine ingredients in a cocktail shaker. Shake vigorously then strain into chilled martini glass.

To make vanilla-infused vodka, combine 1 cup vodka and 2 split vanilla beans in a glass jar, cover; stand for 5 days or until the vodka is infused with vanilla flavor. Discard vanilla beans before using. Frangelico is a hazelnut-flavored liqueur.

dry martini

1½ ounces gin
2 tablespoons dry vermouth
1 cup ice cubes
1 caperberry

prep time 5 minutes
serves 1

1 Combine ingredients in a cocktail shaker. Shake vigorously then strain into chilled martini glass. Garnish with caperberry.

vanilla martini

tip Bartenders frequently use sugar syrup instead of sugar to sweeten drinks because it blends instantly. This recipe makes 1¹/₃ cups and will keep in a screw-top jar in the fridge for up to 2 months.

dry martini

tip The martini is a classic American cocktail that is perhaps the best known of mixed drinks. Famous long before James Bond began requesting his "shaken, not stirred", it was a favorite among many historical legends, including Winston Churchill, Truman Capote, F. Scott Fitzgerald and Ernest Hemingway.

lemon friatto

2 tablespoons citron vodka

2 tablespoons limoncello

1 teaspoon fresh grated orange zest

1 cup ice cubes

3 medium scoops lemon sorbet

prep time 5 minutes

serves 1

1 Combine vodka, limoncello, zest and ice cubes in a cocktail shaker; shake vigorously.

2 Place sorbet in chilled glass; pour limoncello mixture over the sorbet.

manhattan

¼ cup rye whisky

2 tablespoons vermouth rosso

1 cup ice cubes

1 maraschino cherry

prep time 5 minutes

serves 1

1 Combine ingredients in a cocktail shaker. Shake vigorously then strain into a chilled margarita glass.

2 Drop cherry into glass to serve.

lemon friatto

tip Citron vodka is a lemon and lime flavored vodka that contains small amounts of lemon peel. Limoncello is a popular after-dinner drink in Italy, and is usually served ice cold. It is sweet and lemony, but not sour.

manhattan

tip If this cocktail is too sweet, make it a 'dry' Manhattan by substituting dry vermouth for the sweet rosso. You can also add a dash of Angostura bitters for a more classic version of the drink.

frozen mango daiquiri

¼ cup white rum

¼ cup mango liqueur

2 tablespoons fresh lime juice

1 medium ripe mango, peeled, coarsely chopped

1 cup ice cubes

prep time 5 minutes
serves 1

1 Blend or process ingredients until just combined. Pour into glass.

bounty

2 tablespoons baileys irish cream

1 tablespoons kahlúa

1 tablespoons coconut syrup

¼ cup fresh cream

1 cup ice cubes

prep time 5 minutes
serves 1

1 Blend or process ingredients on high speed until combined. Pour into a chilled brandy glass.

Champagne cocktail

2-inch strip orange zest

1 sugar cube

5 drops angostura bitters

2/3 cup chilled Champagne

prep time 5 minutes
serves 1

1 Slice zest thinly.
2 Place sugar cube in champagne glass; top with bitters then Champagne. Garnish with zest.

Use marginally less than 2/3 cup of Champagne for each cocktail and you will be able to make five cocktails from one bottle of Champagne.

fruity Champagne

1/2 medium peach, peeled, coarsely chopped

1 tablespoon fresh lemon juice
dash grenadine

1/3 cup chilled Champagne

prep time 5 minutes
serves 1

1 Blend or process peach until smooth; you need 2 tablespoons of peach puree.
2 Combine peach puree in a champagne glass with lemon juice and grenadine; top with chilled Champagne.

cosmopolitan

1½ ounces vodka
 2 tablespoons cointreau
 4 teaspoons cranberry juice
 2 teaspoons lime juice
 1 cup ice cubes

prep time 5 minutes
serves 1

1 Combine vodka, cointreau, cranberry juice, lime juice and ice in cocktail shaker; shake vigorously. Strain into chilled martini glass.

margarita

1½ ounces tequila
 2 tablespoons fresh lime juice
 2 tablespoons cointreau
 1 cup ice cubes

prep time 5 minutes
serves 1

1 Combine ingredients in a cocktail shaker; shake vigorously. Strain into a salt-rimmed margarita glass.

cosmopolitan

tip This refreshingly tart concoction is a popular summer cocktail that is often referred to simply as a 'cosmo'.

tip Margaritas are always served in salt-rimmed glasses. Mexicans discovered that salt on the tongue calms the fiery flavors in their food. Served with tequila, salt reduces the 'burn'.

margarita

caipirinha

1 lime
2 teaspoons sugar
1½ ounces vodka
½ cup crushed ice

prep time 5 minutes
serves 1

1 Cut lime into eight wedges.
2 Using muddler, crush lime wedges with sugar in cocktail shaker. Add vodka and ice; shake vigorously. Pour into glass.

traditional daiquiri

1½ ounces white rum
2 tablespoons fresh lime juice
1 tablespoon sugar syrup (see page 338)
1 cup ice cubes

prep time 5 minutes
serves 1

1 Combine ingredients in a cocktail shaker; shake vigorously then strain into glass.

caipirinha

traditional daiquiri

tip A muddler is a bartender's tool, used to crush or mash fruits, herbs, and/or spices in the bottom of a glass to release their flavors. Use the end of a small rolling pin or thick wooden spoon handle or pestle if you don't have one.

tip The daiquiri was created in a small Cuban town of the same name by an American engineer, who combined the local spirit (rum) with native limes to make the ultimate pick-me-up after a hot day in the iron mines.

blood orange margarita

2 tablespoons dark tequila

1 ounce lime juice

2 tablespoons blood orange juice

2 tablespoons sugar syrup

1 Combine tequila, juices, sugar syrup and 1 cup ice cubes in cocktail shaker; shake vigorously.

2 Strain into salt-rimmed margarita glass.

prep time 5 minutes

serves 1

pomegranate caipirinha

½ lime

¼ cup vodka

2 tablespoons sugar syrup

4 teaspoons pomegranate juice

1 Cut lime into quarters. Using muddler, crush two lime wedges in cocktail shaker with vodka, sugar syrup and juice. Add 1 cup ice cubes; shake vigorously. Strain into ice-filled 8-ounce old-fashioned glass.

2 Garnish with remaining sliced lime wedges.

See the recipe on page 338 for sugar syrup recipe.

prep time 5 minutes

serves 1

classic bellini

1½ ounces peach nectar

1 teaspoon lime juice

1 tablespoon peach schnapps

½ cup chilled brut sparkling wine

1 Place nectar, juice and schnapps in chilled champagne flute; stir to combine. Top with chilled sparkling wine.

prep time 5 minutes

serves 1

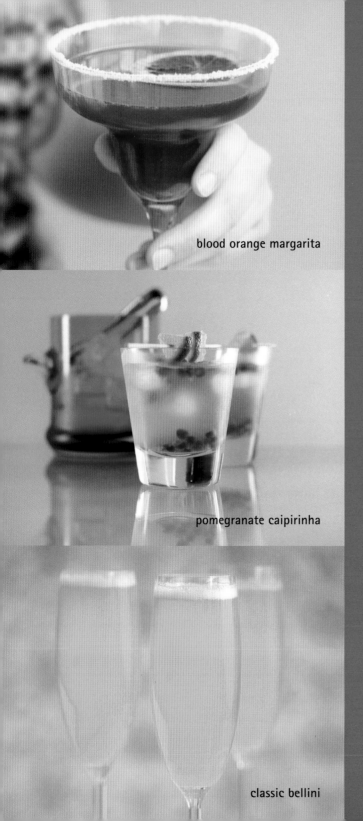

tips Garnish with a slice of blood orange, if you like. This cocktail looks striking with blood oranges but you can use navel oranges instead.

blood orange margarita

tip You can stir in 1 tablespoon pomegranate pulp, if you like, before garnishing with lime.

pomegranate caipirinha

tip This famous cocktail was invented by Guiseppe Cipriani, the founder of Harry's Bar in Venice, Italy. It is traditionally made with white peach puree and sparkling Italian wine (prosecco).

classic bellini

french kiss

2 tablespoons raspberry liqueur
2 tablespoons berry iced tea
½ cup chilled lemonade
    fresh raspberries, to serve

1 Place liqueur and tea in chilled champagne
    glass; stir gently. Top with lemonade.
2 Garnish with raspberries.

prep time 5 minutes
serves 1

white russian

½ cup ice cubes
2 tablespoons vodka
2 tablespoons kahlúa
2 tablespoons fresh cream

1 Place ice in glass; pour vodka then kahlúa over
    ice. Gently pour cream into glass over the back
    of a tablespoon so cream floats (do not stir).

prep time 5 minutes
serves 1

black russian

½ cup ice cubes
2 tablespoons vodka
2 tablespoons kahlúa
½ cup cola

1 Place ice in glass; pour vodka then kahlúa over
    ice. Top with cola.

prep time 5 minutes
serves 1

salty dog

1 cup ice cubes
1½ ounces vodka
½ cup fresh grapefruit juice

prep time 5 minutes
serves 1

1 Place ice in salt-rimmed glass; add vodka then juice. Garnish with strips of grapefruit zest.

sea breeze

½ cup cranberry juice
2 tablespoons ruby red grapefruit juice
1½ ounces vodka
1 cup ice cubes

prep time 5 minutes
serves 1

1 Combine ingredients in glass; stir well.

ANGOSTURA BITTERS used mainly in drinks. Its recipe is a closely guarded secret, but it is made of many herbs and spices.

ARROWROOT a starch used mostly for thickening. Cornflour can be substituted but will not give as clear a glaze.

ARUGULA a peppery-tasting green leaf. Baby arugula leaves are smaller and less peppery.

BABA GHANOUSH a roasted eggplant dip.

BEANS

fava also known as broad beans. Fresh and frozen forms should be peeled twice (discarding both the outer long green pod and the beige-green tough inner shell).

cannellini small white bean similar to great northern, navy or haricot, for which they can be substituted.

green also known as French or string beans (although the tough string they once had has generally been bred out of them), this long thin fresh bean is consumed in its entirety.

refried pinto or borlotti beans, having been cooked twice—first boiled, then mashed and fried.

white some recipes in this book may simply call for 'white beans', a generic term we use for dried or canned cannellini, haricot, navy or great northern beans.

BLOOD ORANGE a virtually seedless citrus fruit with blood-red-streaked zest and flesh; sweet, non-acidic, salmon-colored pulp and juice with slight strawberry or raspberry overtones.

BREAD

brioche rich, yeast-risen french bread made with butter and eggs. Available from better bakeries.

ciabatta in Italian, the word means 'slipper', which is the traditional shape of this popular white bread with a crisp crust.

focaccia a flat italian-style bread, also available as rolls. Made from a basic yeast dough; the top is dimpled and brushed with oil to keep the bread moist. Other toppings, such as salt or herbs, may be sprinkled on top.

lavash flat, unleavened bread of Mediterranean origin.

melba toasts (mini toasts) traditionally a very thin-sliced bread that has had the crusts removed before it is toasted.

pita also known as lebanese bread. This wheat-flour pocket bread is sold in large, flat pieces that separate into two rounds.

sourdough so-named, not because it's sour in taste, but because it's made by using a small amount of 'starter dough', which contains a yeast culture, mixed into flour and water. Part of the resulting dough is then saved to use as the starter dough next time.

tortillas thin, round unleavened bread originating in Mexico. Two kinds are available, one made from wheat flour and the other from corn.

turkish comes in long flat loaves as well as individual rounds. Made from wheat flour and sprinkled with sesame seeds or black onion seeds.

BREADCRUMBS

packaged fine-textured, crunchy, purchased white breadcrumbs.

stale one- or two-day-old bread made into crumbs by blending or processing.

BROCCOLINI a cross between broccoli and chinese kale; milder and sweeter than broccoli. Each long stem is topped by a loose floret that closely resembles broccoli; from stem to floret, broccolini is completely edible.

BUTTER use salted or unsalted (sweet) butter; 1 stick is equal to 4 ounces (8 tablespoons) of butter.

unsalted or 'sweet' butter, simply has no added salt. You can use regular butter in most cakes and baking, but it's best stick to unsalted butter when it's called for in a recipe.

CAJUN SEASONING a blend of herbs and spices including paprika, basil, onion, fennel, thyme, cayenne and tarragon.

CAPERS the gray-green buds of a warm climate (usually Mediterranean) shrub; sold either dried and salted or pickled in a vinegar brine. Baby capers, those picked early, are smaller, fuller-flavored and more expensive than the full-sized ones. Capers should be rinsed well before using.

CARDAMOM can be purchased in pod, seed or ground form. Has a distinctive aromatic, sweetly rich flavor and is one of the world's most expensive spices.

CELERIAC tuberous root with a brown skin, white flesh and a celery-like flavor. Its soft, velvety flesh has the creaminess of potato when mashed, with a subtle celery flavor.

CHEESE

blue brie mould-treated cheese mottled with blue veining.

bocconcini walnut-sized, fresh, baby mozzarella.

brie often referred to as the 'queen of cheeses'. Has a bloomy white rind and a smooth creamy centre that becomes runnier as it ripens.

cream cheese commonly known as Philadelphia or Philly, a soft cows-milk cheese.

feta Greek in origin; a crumbly textured goat's or sheep's milk cheese with a sharp, salty taste.

fontina a smooth, firm cows-milk cheese with a nutty taste and brown or red rind; an ideal melting or grilling cheese.

goat made from goat milk, has an earthy, strong taste; available in both soft and firm textures, in various shapes and sizes, sometimes rolled in ash or herbs.

haloumi a firm, cream-colored sheep-milk cheese matured in brine; somewhat like a minty, salty feta in flavor. Can be grilled or fried, briefly, without breaking down. Should be eaten while still warm as it becomes tough and rubbery on cooling.

mascarpone a buttery-rich, cream-like cheese made from cows milk. Is ivory-colored, soft and delicate, with the texture of softened butter.

pecorino the generic Italian name for cheeses made from sheep milk. It's a hard, white to pale yellow cheese; if you can't find it, use Parmesan cheese.

CHICKEN To ensure chicken is thoroughly cooked, insert a meat thermometer in the thickest piece (not touching the bone). If cooking a whole chicken, insert thermometer in the thigh. Chicken is done when the internal temperature reaches 165˚F.

CHILES available in many types and sizes. Use rubber gloves when seeding and chopping fresh chiles as they can burn your skin. Removing seeds and membranes lessens the heat level.

flakes deep-red, dehydrated chilli slices and whole seeds.

green any unripened chilli; also some varieties that are ripe when green, such as jalapeño, habanero, poblano or serrano.

long red available both fresh and dried; a generic term used for any moderately hot, long, thin chilli.

red thai also known as 'scuds'; small, bright red and very hot.

CHOCOLATE

dark eating also known as semi-sweet; made of a high percentage of cocoa liquor and cocoa butter, and a little added sugar.

milk the most popular eating chocolate, mild and very sweet; similar in make-up to dark with the difference being the addition of milk solids.

white contains no cocoa solids but derives its sweet flavor from cocoa butter. Sensitive to heat, so watch carefully if melting.

CHORIZO made of coarsely ground pork and seasoned with garlic and chiles.

CILANTRO also known as chinese parsley; a green-leafed herb with a pungent flavor. Also known as coriander when available ground or as seeds, though coriander cannot be substituted for fresh cilantro.

COCONUT MILK not the liquid found inside the fruit, which is called coconut water, but the diluted liquid from the second pressing of the white flesh of a mature coconut (the first pressing produces coconut cream). Available in cans and cartons at most supermarkets.

COUSCOUS a fine, grain-like cereal product made from semolina. A semolina dough is sieved then dehydrated to produce minuscule pellets of couscous; it is rehydrated by steaming, or with the addition of a warm liquid, and swells to three or four times its original size.

CREAM we use fresh heavy cream unless otherwise noted.

crème fraîche mature fermented cream with a slightly tangy, nutty flavor and velvety texture.

GELATIN we use dried (powdered) gelatin in this book; it's also available in sheet form known as leaf gelatin. A thickening agent made from either collagen, a protein found in animal connective tissue and bones, or certain algae (agar-agar). Three teaspoons of dried gelatin is about the same as four gelatin leaves. The two types are interchangable but leaf gelatin gives a much clearer mixture than dried gelatin; it's perfect in dishes where appearance really matters.

GHEE clarified butter with the milk solids removed; this fat can be heated to high temperatures without burning.

GINGER known as green or root ginger; the thick root of a tropical plant.

GOLDEN SYRUP a by-product of refined sugar cane; pure maple syrup or honey can be substituted.

HARISSA *see pastes.*

HORSERADISH a commercially prepared condiment, which is preserved grated horseradish root.

HUMMUS a Middle-Eastern salad or dip made from garlic, chickpeas, lemon juice and tahini (sesame seed paste).

KITCHEN STRING made of a natural product, such as cotton or hemp, so it neither affects the flavour of the food it's tied around nor melts when heated.

LEMON PEPPER SEASONING a blend of crushed black pepper, lemon, herbs and spices.

LENTILS (red, brown, yellow) dried pulses often identified by and named after their color.

MALIBU coconut-flavored rum.

MIRIN sweet rice wine used in Japanese cooking; not to be confused with sake.

MIXED SALAD LEAVES
mixed baby leaves, also sold
as salad mix, mesclun or gourmet
salad mix; a mix of assorted
young lettuce and other green
leaves.

MORTADELLA a cured sausage
made of ground pork that is
mashed into a paste then flavored
with spices.

MUDDLER a bartender's tool,
used to crush, or mash, fruits,
herbs, and/or spices in the
bottom of a glass to release their
flavour. Use the end of a small
rolling pin or thick wooden spoon
handle, or a pestle, if you don't
have one.

MUSHROOMS cremini Light
to dark-brown mushrooms
with a full-bodied flavor.

oyster grey-white mushrooms
shaped like a fan. Has a smooth
texture and subtle, oyster-like
flavor.

shiitake, fresh are also
known as chinese black,
golden oak or forest mushrooms.
Although cultivated, they are
large and meaty and have the
earthiness and taste of wild
mushrooms.

MUSTARD
dijon also called French. Pale
brown, creamy, distinctively
flavored, mild French mustard.

wholegrain also known as
seeded. A French-style coarse-
grain mustard made from crushed
mustard seeds and Dijon-style
french mustard.

OLIVES
green those harvested before
fully ripened and are, as a rule,
denser and more bitter than
their black relatives.

kalamata small, sharp-tasting,
brine-cured black olives.

sicilian dark olive green in color;
smooth and fine-skinned with
a crisp and crunchy bite, and a
piquant, buttery flavor.

ONION
pickling or cocktail onions; are
baby brown or white onions.

red also known as spanish,
red spanish or bermuda onion.

scallion an immature onion
picked before the bulb has formed,
having a long, bright-green edible
stalk.

shallots also called french
shallots; small, brown-skinned,
elongated members of the onion
family.

PANCETTA an Italian unsmoked
bacon; pork belly is cured in
salt and spices then rolled into a
sausage shape and dried.

PAPAYA large, pear-shaped red-
orange tropical fruit. Can also be
used unripe (green) in Asian
cooking.

PARSLEY FLAT-LEAF also known
as or italian parsley.

PASTES
harissa a moroccan paste
made from dried chiles, cumin,
garlic, oil and caraway seeds;
available from Middle-Eastern
food stores and some
supermarkets.

red curry probably the most
popular curry paste; a medium
heat blend of chiles garlic, onion,
lemon grass, spice and galangal.

tandoori a medium heat paste
consisting of garlic, tamarind,
ginger, coriander, chiles and other
spices.

tikka a medium/mild paste
consisting of chiles, coriander,
cumin, lentil flour, garlic, ginger,
turmeric, fennel, pepper, cloves,
cinnamon and cardamom.

yellow curry one of the mildest
pastes; similar to Indian curry
paste due to the use of mild
yellow chiles and fresh turmeric.

PATTY-PAN SQUASH also known
as crookneck; a round, slightly flat
summer squash yellow to pale-
green in color with a scalloped edge.

PEPPERCORNS
canned green soft, under-ripe
berry preserved in brine and sold
in cans. It has a fresh flavour
that's less pungent than the berry
in its other forms.

peppercorns, mixed dried a mix
of dried pink, white and black
peppercorns.

PINE NUTS also known as
pignoli; not a nut but a small,
cream-colored kernel from
pine cones. They are best
toasted before use to bring
out the flavor.

POLENTA also known as
cornmeal; a flour-like cereal made
of dried corn (maize)
and sold ground in different
textures. Also the name of
the dish made from it.

POMEGRANATE fruit of a
large bush native to the Middle-
East, although it is now grown in
other regions around the world. A
dark-red, leathery-skinned fruit
about the size of
an orange filled with hundreds of
seeds (pulp), each wrapped
in an edible lucent- crimson jelly-
like pulp having a tangy sweet-
sour flavour.

PORK To ensure pork is
thoroughly cooked, insert a meat
thermometer in the thickest piece
(not touching the bone). Pork is
done when the internal
temperature reaches 145°F. Let
rest for 5 minutes before serving.

PROSCIUTTO unsmoked Italian
ham; salted, air-cured and aged, it
is usually eaten uncooked.

RED CURRANT JELLY a preserve
made from red currants; used as a
glaze or
in sauces.

RICE
arborio small round-grain rice;
well suited to absorb a large
amount of liquid, especially good
in risottos.

basmati a white, fragrant long-
grained rice. Wash several times
before cooking.

jasmine a fragrant long-grained
white rice; long-grain white rice
can be substituted, but will not
taste the same.

long-grain white elongated
grain, remains separate when
cooked; most popular steaming
rice in Asia.

SAFFRON THREADS available in
strands or ground form; imparts a
yellow-orange color to food once

infused. Quality varies greatly; the best is the most expensive spice in the world. Store in the freezer.

SALAMI cured sausages heavily seasoned with garlic and spices.

SAUCES

barbecue spicy, tomato-based sauce used to marinate, baste or as an accompaniment.

char siu a Chinese barbecue sauce made from sugar, water, salt, fermented soy bean paste, honey, soy sauce, malt syrup and spices. It can be found at most supermarkets.

cranberry a packaged product made of cranberries cooked in sugar syrup.

hoisin a thick, sweet and spicy Chinese paste made from salted fermented soya beans, onions and garlic.

oyster Asian in origin, this rich, brown sauce is made from oysters and their brine, cooked with salt and soy sauce, and thickened with starches.

piri–piri (peri-peri) the hot West African sauce made from dried and soaked piri-piri chiles. Is available in bottles from delis and supermarkets.

plum a thick, sweet and sour dipping sauce made from plums, vinegar, sugar, chiles and spices.

soy made from fermented soya beans. Several variations are available in most supermarkets and Asian food stores.

sweet chili a reasonably mild sauce made from red chiles, sugar, garlic and vinegar.

tamari a thick, dark sauce made mainly from soy beans. Has a mellow flavor. Available from Asian food stores.

tomato also known as ketchup or catsup; made from tomatoes, vinegar and spices.

worcestershire a dark-brown, thin, spicy sauce made from anchovies, tamarind, molasses and other seasonings.

STAR ANISE a dried star-shaped fruit of a tree native to China. The pods have an astringent anise or licorice flavor. Available whole and ground, it is an essential ingredient in five-spice powder.

SUMAC a purple-red, astringent spice ground from berries growing on shrubs that flourish wild around the Mediterranean; adds a tart, lemony flavor to meats and dips. Available from Middle-Eastern food stores.

japanese soy is an all-purpose low-sodium soy sauce made with more wheat content than its Chinese counterparts. Possibly the best table soy, and the one to choose if you only want one variety.

light soy is a fairly thin, pale, salty tasting sauce; used in dishes where the natural color of the ingredients is to be maintained. Not to be confused with salt-reduced or low-sodium soy sauces.

SWEETENED CONDENSED MILK 60% of the water has been removed; the remaining milk is then sweetened with sugar.

TABBOULEH a Middle-Eastern dish made with bulgur wheat, tomatoes, onions, parsley, mint, olive oil and lemon juice.

TAHINI a rich sesame-seed paste available from Middle-Eastern food stores; most often used in hummus, baba ghanoush and other Lebanese recipes.

TAMARIND a sweet-sour, slightly astringent paste made from the viscous pulp of the seeds of the tamarind tree; can be dried and pressed into the blocks found in Asian food shops.

TZATZIKI Greek yogurt and cucumber dip sometimes containing mint and/or garlic.

VANILLA BEAN dried long, thin pod from a tropical golden orchid; the tiny black seeds impart a luscious vanilla flavor.

VINEGAR

balsamic made from the juice of Trebbiano grapes; is a deep rich brown color with a sweet and sour flavor.

cider (apple cider) made from fermented apples.

malt (brown malt) made from fermented malt and beech shavings.

red wine based on fermented red wine.

rice a colorless vinegar made from fermented rice, sugar and salt. Also known as seasoned rice vinegar.

rice wine made from rice wine lees (the sediment left after fermentation), salt and alcohol.

white made from spirit of cane sugar.

white wine made from white wine.

WASABI an Asian horseradish sold as a powder or paste. Has a hot, pungent taste.

WATERCRESS also known as winter arugla; a peppery green. Highly perishable, so use as soon as possible after purchase.

Index